HOW TO LEAD WITH PURPOSE

LESSONS IN LIFE AND
WORK FROM THE
GLOVES-OFF MENTOR

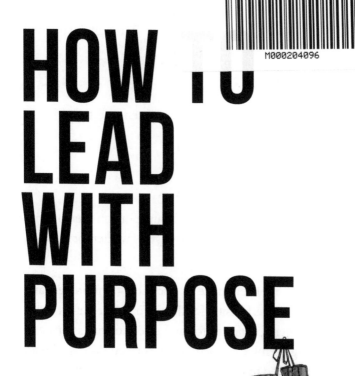

LIAM BLACK

First published in Great Britain by Practical Inspiration Publishing, 2023

© Liam Black, 2023

The moral rights of the author have been asserted

ISBN   9781788604079 (print)
       9781788604093 (epub)
       9781788604086 (mobi)

Every effort has been made to trace copyright holders and to obtain their permission for the use of copyright material. The publisher apologizes for any errors or omissions and would be grateful if notified of any corrections that should be incorporated in future reprints or editions of this book.

Want to bulk-buy copies of this book for your team and colleagues? We can introduce case studies, customize the content and co-brand *How to Lead with Purpose* to suit your business's needs.

Please email info@practicalinspiration.com for more details.

Practical Inspiration
Publishing

This book is dedicated to my grandkids Isabelle, Mia, Finbar and Cormac.

Mentor - noun - A wise and trusted counsellor or teacher willing to advise, support, champion, challenge and connect.

'*A coach has some great questions for your answers. A mentor has some great answers for your questions.*'
Anon

'*Awful week. Didn't take your advice. Fucked up. Need a dose of your gloves-off mentoring. Liam call me asap*'
Text received 14th November 2020, 23.50

Contents

Foreword

At Timpson, business is more than just business. We use our network of more than 2,000 shops across the United Kingdom to build a better and safer society. We have found a pool of extraordinary talent behind prison walls, and we have recruited more than 700 men and women through our training centres in six UK prisons.

We don't just do this because we believe that business has responsibilities that go way beyond what company law dictates. We do what we do because it is good for our business as well as the communities in which we run our shops. Reoffending costs this country £17 billion a year, so keeping people out of jail saves the taxpayer money. It also gets Timpson productive and engaged colleagues who provide great service for our customers, which means they come back and spend more – and so the business makes money.

We were on our own for too many years, and Timpson was ridiculed as a 'soft touch' by the tabloids. But today we see more and more companies realizing the benefits of aligning a social purpose with a business need. Business leaders and entrepreneurs from a wide range of sectors and industries are involved in

Employment Advisory Boards in prisons all over the country. We have to compete for talent in prisons now!

Aligning purpose and business is not easy by any means. Changing the world is not for the faint-hearted or those easily defeated by setbacks. So we must support one another and share our learning, warts and all. This is where Liam's book comes in. It is spot on. It gives straightforward, no-nonsense advice and it will be invaluable to you if you want to make a positive difference in the world through your business and work.

No grand theories, no academic mind games, no pontificating. Just practical, gloves-off, straight-to-the-point advice drawing on Liam's deep experience and hard-won wisdom as founder, chief executive, chair, investor and mentor. Of course it is laced with Liam's trademark wit and humour and there is not one jot of wishful thinking or avoidance.

I have known Liam for more than 15 years and I have valued his counsel and provocations on stage and one to one. I love referring people to Liam for a dose of his gloves-off mentoring because I know they will always benefit enormously from his wisdom, challenge and compassion.

In the future, whenever someone asks me 'How do I avoid making mistakes and make better decisions?' I will point them to this book.

James Timpson
Chief Executive of Timpson and Chairman of Prison Reform Trust

Introduction

Clarity and courage

Friday, 7am. I'm about to leave the house and go for a run along Tring Canal when the phone rings. It's Jane. We've been working together for six months.

She's in her late thirties and deep into her first CEO role, in a high-pressure tech-related social enterprise.

'Can you talk?'

'Of course. Hang on,' I say, as I take off my windcheater, plug in my earphones and sit down on the bottom stair. 'Go ahead.'

She'd gone to bed at 10pm and been woken in the wee hours by her three-year-old boy, who had puked all over the landing. Afterwards she just couldn't get back to sleep; her mind was boiling with anxiety about today's board meeting, at which she is introducing her first long-term strategic plan to a demanding set of investors and directors.

We do some breathing exercises and then I ask her to talk me through the meeting strategy we worked on the previous week. By 7.40am she is calm and back in her authority.

I remind her that she's done the work to be ready for today, that she has the full backing of the board and they are keen for her to succeed. 'This is what you wanted, Jane. This is what it feels like when you want to change the world and that collides with running a fast-growing business and being accountable to some serious people.'

She ends the call and I go for my run.

At 5pm she phones again, breathless, hurried, dashing out of the office on her way to Waterloo.

'Liam, it went really well. They're on board with all of it. Talk next week. Bye.'

And she's gone.

Further, faster

Jane was in a cool job that many would kill for, the female CEO pioneering the way for talented, ambitious women, invited to speak at endless high-profile events. And yet, in that first year she frequently felt that it was all about to fall apart at any moment. The cavernous gap between how it looked (and how she really wanted it to be) and how it actually felt threatened to swallow her. That's what leadership in the real world is like, isn't it?

I love working with leaders like Jane. Some are embedded in multinational corporations, some have left that world to start their own purpose-driven businesses in finance, climate or healthcare, and still others are leading in the charity and public sectors.

The people who ask me to mentor them tell me they do so because of my no-nonsense and direct style and my experiences over many years in organisations of all types trying to make a positive difference in the world.

Over four decades I have been a volunteer, employee, CEO, business founder, non-executive director, executive chairman, investor, mentor and adviser. I don't present myself as any sort of leadership guru – far too many of those aren't there? – and I don't have any formal mentoring or coaching qualifications. I'm just endlessly curious about people and I love to be around smart, ambitious leaders who want to do good shit.

My first significant leadership role – with real money and people's jobs on the line – was as director in the north of England and Northern Ireland for a funding agency called Crisis. I was in my early thirties and responsible for raising lots of cash and giving it away to projects offering support and care to homeless people. We opened night shelters for the street homeless and made a point of backing pioneering and ground-breaking work which other funders wouldn't go near in the early 90s.[1]

I gave a grant of £180,000 to a Liverpool-based organisation called the Furniture Resource Centre (FRC) founded in 1988 to help families in poverty get their hands on decent furniture to make a home. I joined the board and, with the founders Nic Frances and Robbie Davison, was part of the transformation from an organisation wholly reliant on the kindness and whims of strangers to a very different one. FRC

---

[1] For example, we gave Manchester's Albert Kennedy Trust its first grant.

re-launched in 1994 as a social business, aspiring to make its money and achieve its mission by trading goods and services across the north-west and beyond. Our goal was to break the debilitating reliance on free money from foundations and the state.

I took over as CEO in 1998, the year after Tony Blair had been elected prime minister for the first time and the words 'social entrepreneur' and 'social enterprise' began to be talked about in government policy circles. I spoke in Whitehall at the launch of Blair's first social enterprise strategy. Around this time I co-founded the Social Enterprise Coalition and I travelled the country banging the drum for this brave new world of entre-preneurial-driven social change.[2]

FRC gave birth to numerous spin-offs including the Cat's Pyjamas, a consultancy and events business focussed on helping people who wanted to follow our example on the banks of the Mersey and shift culture from 'charity' to 'social business'. With my co-founder Jeremy Nicholls we wrote a book called *There's No Business like Social Business* and went to the House of Commons to launch it. The Cat's PJs ran events as far afield as Seattle and Cape Town. We had a ball.

In 2004 I left Liverpool for London to join the Jamie Oliver Group as CEO, for four years riding the

---

[2] Now known as Social Enterprise UK.

helter-skelter of a celebrity-driven brand. I will tell you more about that in Chapter Three.

At 48, with Jess Stack and Adrian Simpson, I co-founded a company called Wavelength and, for the next decade, as Chief Encouragement Officer, helped to grow a highly successful globally networked leadership development and executive education company. Over those 10 years I was in and out of the C-Suites of companies such as Lego, Dyson, Google, the BBC and Unilever. I travelled the world, running events in rural areas of Bangladesh and the bright shiny citadels of Silicon Valley's surveillance capitalists.

I somehow fitted in time to sit on the board of a London-based foundation and discovered how easy it is to waste other people's money on 'innovation'. It was there that my suspicion of anyone calling themselves a 'disruptive innovator' or, horror, a 'thought leader' really bedded in.

In 2014 I published my second book *The Social Entrepreneur's A to Z*.

I exited Wavelength in 2018 and paid off the mortgage. These days, I spend my time on a portfolio of interesting and useful work and finding ways to entertain my four grandchildren. I sit on the investment committee of a 10-year capital growth fund called

Impact Ventures UK. We back entrepreneurs who want to change things and I'm on the board of one of the portfolio companies, Togetherall, a global online peer-to-peer platform for people isolated by anxiety and depression.

In 2021 I took over as Executive Chairman at The Conduit, a global community of entrepreneurs, social innovators, investors and all-round good eggs, based at our lovely building in Covent Garden. I also host gatherings at the Forward Institute of senior leaders from business, the military, police and non-profits, people grappling with complex problems for which there are no straightforward solutions.

Honestly, I have made every mistake in the book as a leader and still wince at some of my failures and errors of judgement. Plenty of times naivety, macho arrogance, resentment, fear, obstinacy got the better of me. But I have learned a lot about the critical importance of organisational culture, curating winning teams, healthy boards, personal mastery and humility (tricky one for me) – and that revenue is vanity, profit is sanity and cash is king.

I am in the enabling part of life, and my mentoring work is very much core to this, making available my experiences, my wisdom, leadership scar tissue, networks and connectivity to help others go further, faster.

About this book

I wrote *How to Lead with Purpose* to encourage anyone who wants to lead in ways that make the world better; to do work that has meaning beyond the bottom line; to leave their mark and experience agency and fulfilment.

I have used my clients' stories (with their full permission) and a few of my own to draw out some of the lessons we are learning about how to align purpose and leadership; how to make a difference in the world and look after ourselves.

I have divided *How to Lead with Purpose* into two parts. The first, *Making a difference*, covers our motivations – *Why do you want to change the world?*; the courage and self-belief required to follow your social purposes; how to align what you want to do with the best place to do it; and how you understand and use the leadership roles you have to make a difference.

Staying alive, the second part, deals with the bullshit, bullying and opposition you'll encounter and takes a hard look at the risks of letting a desire to be part of making positive social change damage your relationships and personal well-being. I devote

Chapter Seven to the sexist crap which women have to face.

Each chapter ends with some gloves-off questions and provocations so that this book gets *you* thinking and taking some action and not just enjoying a pleasant read!

There is nothing much original or new in this little book. Samuel Johnson said that we need to be reminded much more than we need to be instructed, and he was right. In the maelstrom of leadership, it is perilously easy to forget the basics. Most leaders know what they need to do to improve their organisations but choose not to do it. Much easier to listen to a blind mountain climber or Silicon Valley guru talk about how you too can be a world champion than it is to get stuck into the grind of incremental change back at the office.

'Purpose' is up there with 'innovation', 'sustainability' and 'diversity' as a leadership subject about which so much bullshit and wishful thinking is spoken and written, so I promise you no BS in these pages. I assume you are a grown-up who does not need to be flattered or spoon-fed glib conclusions or advice.

When I mentor, I take off the gloves and give it to people straight, speaking plainly, calling out wishful or lazy thinking, denial and avoidance. So *How to Lead with Purpose* isn't a collection of inspiring airbrushed stories and I have not written the book to inspire you

9

particularly. My intention is that you will find it *useful* as you figure out how to make a difference in the world through your work and how to deal with setbacks and resistance and overcome the ways in which we undermine ourselves.

You won't find any grand theories about leadership or change. I don't know (or care) if leaders are born or made. What I do know is that the pressure of leadership reveals the truth about one's deepest held values and beliefs, much more than it forms them.

Crisis exposes the kind of leaders we really are. Covid-19 was a truth serum that every leader had to swallow. There was no hiding place for any of us. The pandemic exposed many business leaders for the 'me first', money-grabbing, selfish men and women they have always been. But others, in unprecedented times and with no operating manual to consult, showed extraordinary solidarity with their employees, revealing a degree of practical empathy that people won't forget.

Clarity and courage

At root, I offer those I mentor help with two things: clarity and courage. I try to help them get clear about what it is they really want to achieve with their leadership, to cut through the noise around them and in their heads, to get to what's really going on for them.

I work too on helping to build their courage. It requires sustained bravery and resilience to go for what you want, especially if what you want involves ending homelessness, cutting out plastics from your global supply chain, changing an organisation's culture, leaving the well-paid job to set up your own business or ending that 10-year business partnership.

Typically, people seek me out when they are entering times of change and challenge, sensing the need for someone to walk alongside them as they find their way through unknown territory.

For example, Myriam Sidibe, a senior executive at Unilever at the time, approached me about mentoring when she had just been awarded a senior fellowship at the Harvard Kennedy School. Myriam is a well-known figure in the corporate sustainability world and is perhaps best known for helping to create World Handwashing Day, which has now reached over a billion people.

Leaving her family behind in Nairobi to settle in Boston for a year, Myriam knew that the experience would be tough. Beyond those 12 months in the US lay the dilemma about whether to stay at Unilever or, after 15 years, leave the corporate life support machine and strike out on her own to create a platform on the back of the book she would write.[3]

'Mentoring was crucial for me during the time of transition between a corporation, academia and setting up my own business,' Myriam told me. 'Having a mentor gave me the confidence to stay the course and also sometimes the push required to stop thinking about my own little self and keep going back to my purpose even when the road ahead wasn't clear.'

Myriam, a mother of three, knew the time away on this amazing, once-in-a-lifetime opportunity, would be lonely and frightening at times. 'I knew I couldn't go through this transition alone and stay sane as a mother, a wife and a professional.'

Myriam asked me not to hold back, to take the gloves off. 'I needed someone to help me assess my options honestly and to help me not get mired by my own self-pity and self-inflicted dramas.'

If this book helps you become clearer about what you want, figure out why you are feeling unhappy or anxious in your current leadership role, and find a bit more courage to go for what you really want, then it will have been well worth the writing.

Let's start.

---

[3] Myriam's excellent book *Brands on a Mission: How to Achieve Social Impact in Business* is published by Routledge.

Part One

Making a difference

Chapter One

So, you want to change the world...

C aroline is sick and tired of the 'profit only' motive of the businesses where she has worked since graduation.[4] She's jacked in her well-paid job with a multinational corporation and, with enough savings to keep the family afloat for two years if they are careful, she intends to start up a fintech business to tackle poverty in the UK.

Caroline is telling me all this over a coffee in a central London café. We've been connected by a mutual friend and we are both enjoying our first mentoring blind date. This 40-year-old woman is very articulate

---

[4] For obvious reasons I have changed most of the names of the clients whose stories I use in this book. All direct quotes used have been confirmed and agreed with the people quoted.

and obviously really bright. Words tumble out of her as she speaks about the heady mixture of relief, excitement, fear and uncertainty she is experiencing. She tells me about her former bosses who think she's either inspirational or insane to walk away from a rising career in investment banking.

Her husband Andrew is sceptical though and worries that her decision is the sign of early-onset mid-life crisis. He has told her she has a year to make this work because he doesn't want all their savings blown. Their three kids and security – not risk-taking and changing the world – are his priority. 'Our world, our family, is the most important thing,' he has told her.

As we start our second cups of coffee, Caroline takes out her notebook and sketches the shape of her business idea and how it will positively help people on low incomes who've become trapped in debt by unscrupulous lenders. Over the coming two years I will become very familiar with Caroline's carefully constructed flow charts and Venn diagrams.

Between slurps of cappuccino, she tells me she wants me to advise her on starting a business, how to avoid stupid mistakes, to introduce her to angels and impact investors, to build a board when the time is right and help shape her story to the world. She flicks through her notebook to show me some names and company logos she's been working on. Her enthusiasm and energy are off the charts. It's easy to see how this charisma and drive propelled her up the corporate ladder.

Eventually, she stops talking and looks straight at me. 'So, okay Liam, what do you think? Give it to me straight. Am I mad? Can I be a social entrepreneur?'

'I have one question for you,' I reply. 'Why are you doing this?'

Caroline takes a deep breath, exhales loudly and looks past me out at the busy Covent Garden street. After a long pause, she's back in the room with me. 'I want to do something with purpose, I want to do work that means something, that matters. I just want to make a fucking difference.'

In this chapter we'll look at what motivates this desire to make a difference and why it is so important that you understand – as best you can – what it is that is driving you and how your reasons for why you do what you do change over time.

The 'Why?' question is the first one I ask of those who want me to mentor them.

'Why do you care about inequality?'

'Why is it your job to tackle climate change?'

'Why is purpose more important than profit to you?'

'Why do you think you can make the difference in the world you say you want to?'

'Why are you so special? Maybe you'll make things worse!'

The many 'whys'

I have heard many and varied answers to the question of 'Why?' over my years of mentoring.

For some, purpose is driven by anger at injustice and inequality, especially if that has been experienced first-hand. Ishmael who still burns with the shame and anger he experienced when he was a boy and his family were shunted from one crappy temporary accommodation to another around the north-west of England after his father lost his job. Or Mary who will not rest until racism is rooted out of the workplace.

For some of those I've mentored their 'why' is rooted in religious conviction. Steve took on a failing charity for the homeless and the very hard yards of reforming it, because for him that was the way to give expression to his strong Christian faith.

Others are continuing a journey started by their parents or, conversely, they are consciously rejecting the values of their upbringing by challenging the status quo.

Older people I have mentored sometimes talk about a guilty conscience after a successful career piling up money and assets. They want to do something to address the inequalities of a system that has richly rewarded them for their hard work and obedience to the prevailing norms of business.

For the children of the seriously rich who have inherited wealth ('the lucky sperm club' as one young member of it described it to me) there is a sense of obligation tinged with guilt to use their luck and privilege to make a difference or give something back.[5]

There are those who answer the 'why' question with the simple answer that they want to make the world a better place for their children and grandchildren. It's about legacy.

Some relish the intellectual challenge and adventure of tackling some of the world's most complex and intractable problems such as climate change and world poverty. As a battle-hardened social entrepreneur once put it to me, 'It's bloody hard, Liam, but what problem worth cracking isn't bloody hard?'

---

[5] There is another book to be written about the complicated motivations of the children of the seriously wealthy.

Karen Lynch gave up a well-paid job with Barclays Bank to take on the turnaround of the bottled water social enterprise Belu, which in 2010 was close to collapse with huge debts. Now a well-known and influential figure in the UK social enterprise world and an adviser to the government on its small business policy, Karen dedicated 10 years of her life to building a successful business which would donate millions to water projects around the world. Why? 'It's complicated isn't it? There's no one thing. I have always had a hatred of waste – of time, money, people's talent and in the bank there was just so much of this.'

Karen didn't have a road to Damascus conversion to Changing The World. A serious illness put her out of action and she was confined to bed. 'I had my "life's too short" moment and began asking myself "if the next job was my last job what would I do?"'

Karen's very supportive husband told her to go and find it. 'I considered becoming a vicar, an organic pig farmer, retraining as a midwife. My husband "actively coached" me away from these options!'

She happened to see an ad in *The Guardian* for a consultancy gig at Belu and, having never heard the words 'social enterprise' or 'social entrepreneur', applied. And so began a decade of hard work and inspirational transformation. 'Why Belu? It was about reducing waste, being able to bring my ferociously commercial instincts to bear on a meaningful challenge. To be honest, I also liked the fact we supported water projects in Africa. I had travelled a lot there and my dad did his national service in Kenya in the fifties.' There's never just one reason for doing the work we do is there?

If you are reading this book you probably aspire to put a socially beneficial purpose at the centre of your work and creativity. So, what is your why, reader?

Understanding your motivation is critical because any commitment you make to changing how things are – in business, politics, anywhere – will soon encounter resistance and hostility, overt and hidden, from those for whom the current systems work very well thank you and, perhaps more painfully, from those close to you unwilling to pay the price of reduced income or disrupted family life.

A glib, shallow self-knowledge about why you are doing what you are doing will crumble quickly in the face of opposition or realisation of the scale of the job to be done. 'He who has a why,' observed Nietzsche, 'can endure any how.'

Caroline wants to take on the financial services industry whose leaders profit mightily from a grotesquely deformed system. They are not going to roll over in awe of her decision to step off and start up her own business to take them on.

Muhammad Yunus, founder of Bangladesh's Grameen Bank and social entrepreneur extraordinaire, believes that people want meaning in their lives and that the only true meaning comes from doing your part to make a better world. 'Humans have an instinctive, natural desire to make life better for their fellow human beings,' he has written. 'Given the chance, people would prefer to live in a world without poverty, disease, ignorance and needless suffering.'[6] I think he's right. Or perhaps more accurately, I want to believe he's right.

Caroline and I have spent many hours talking about what makes her tick and why leaving her well-paid, high-status job to embrace the uncertainty and back-breaking work of starting her 'tech for good' business aligns with her deepest sense of a meaningful life.

Her motivations are a potent blend of anger at the injustice of a system she knows intimately, intellectual excitement at the challenge of inventing new products and platforms to reach underserved markets, and a deep desire to create something her children will be proud their mum built.

In her really candid moments, Caroline speaks about the future pleasure of proving wrong those who

---

[6] Muhammad Yunus, *Creating A World Without Poverty* (PublicAffairs, 2007, page 37).

think she's made a bad career move. Never underestimate the power of the 'fuck you!' in a social entrepreneur's motivations!

Zealotry and daddy issues

If you'd stopped me in my activist, demo-going, anti-racist twenties and asked me why I was doing all that rather than finding a Proper Job With A Pension, I would probably have given you an answer blending liberation theology and its 'option for the poor' (Gustavo Guttierez, Dorothy Day, Oscar Romero) with left-wing politics (Noam Chomsky, Saul Alinsky) and a bright green splash of Irish republicanism.

No doubt these were all strong influences on me and I was a passionate devotee; at times, I fear, a zealot. But with the benefit of some 40 years' hindsight, looking back at that needy, driven, contradictory young man, I see so clearly that a core part of what was driving him – me – was the seeking of approval from an absent father. If I could change the world, maybe he'd notice me. Long story, for another time.[7]

The roots of what drive us are tangled and often unclear – especially to ourselves. Life, as misery guts

---

[7] Show me a male social entrepreneur and I'll show you a man with daddy issues!

Sören Kierkegaard wrote, has to be lived forward but can only be understood backwards, and that is doubly so for those who opt for a life dedicated to a social purpose. What we believed was driving the decisions we took at 25 looks very different from the vantage points of 45 or 55.

John Elkington is in his seventies and remains as active and agitated about the state of the world as he ever was. John is a leading figure in the world of climate change and sustainability and the author of umpteen books including *The Power of Unreasonable People*, an influential contribution to the field of social entrepreneurship.[8] John coined the phrases 'triple bottom line', 'green consumer' and 'people, profit, planet'. He has spoken everywhere worth speaking, from the UN to the World Economic Forum, and has been consulted by (and clashed with) CEOs across industries and sectors. No event on corporate sustainability is complete without a John Elkington keynote provocation.

John was that voice crying in the wilderness for years, warning that systems collapse lay ahead and profound disruptive change must be confronted.

---

[8] John Elkington and Pamela Hartigan, *The Power of Unreasonable People: How Social Entrepreneurs Create Markets that Change the World* (Harvard Business School Publishing, 2008).

Today he is a sustainability rock star but, objectively, hasn't he failed?

When I spoke to him for this book I asked him what the future looks like. 'A screaming nightmare. That future is here though, isn't it? Floods and fires everywhere. 20% of wetlands burned. Only 3% of the world's animal life is wild.'

What keeps him going? What's his 'why'?

John is rightly wary of glib sloganizing or amateur psychologizing. 'I don't know, really, why I do what I do. Who knows how things would have gone had my life been different? But, at the core, there is this sense that we must increasingly take into account the interests of future generations of all life in everything that we do.'

Clearly he loves what he does ('I can't imagine retiring'), and being part of something bigger than himself seems to lie at the heart of why he has committed himself to changing a world that refuses to change quickly enough in the face of the epochal challenges which are upon us. 'I do accept that I may be delusional,' he tells me. 'Behind everything I do is an understanding that we may crash and burn as a civilisation.'

Both his father and grandfather were fighter pilots who bequeathed to John a warrior element. 'I like a good set-to – long as I don't get killed!' A childhood spent following his father's military career around the world left John with an enduring sense of displacement, at odds with the world, an 'anywhere', with a ferocious curiosity and the willingness to live in ambiguity and contradiction. 'For most of my life I have tried to learn new things, never knowing where that will take me. Perhaps I'm addicted to uncertainty?' Looking back, he sees that he forced the many organisations he co-founded to remain unstable, always ready to change, freeing them to make it up as they went along.

He has targeted what Bill Sharpe has called 'pockets of the future', often to be found where science and economics overlap, and has always discovered enough people, grassroots activists as well as corporate leaders, who shared his sense of urgency. 'Being part of change is always exciting but in there too is guilt about what Homo sapiens is doing and a bloody-mindedness about not giving up... I'm into my seventies and I've been working at this for 50 years, but I think my career's just starting.'

For John the next 10 to 15 years are going to be the most exciting, challenging and politically dangerous of his entire working life. 'We know what needs to be done and there is a sense of urgency building all around. Now really is our time. It really is now or never.'

Luxury beliefs?

Most of those I mentor, myself and I suspect you, dear reader are in the richest 0.1% of the world's population. We, unlike so many of the Earth's people, do not need to worry too much about money, food, shelter and security. We have the luxury of being able to spend time thinking about whether our work has meaning and purpose beyond simply making a living. For many people the purpose in work is to simply put food on the table and pay the rent doing whatever job they can get.

The impacts of Covid were grotesquely unevenly distributed and the virus mercilessly exploited the inequalities that disfigure Britain. The deliberate run-down of public services in the last 10 years in obedience to the Conservative Party's cult of austerity left many people vulnerable to a pandemic long predicted by scientists and ignored by the rest of us.

But the pandemic did – for a few months at least, in the spring and early summer of 2020 – force us to see who is really adding value to society in their work and to acknowledge that this is utterly unconnected to financial reward.

It wasn't the country's hedge fund managers, PR consultants or corporate lawyers that we turned out on our doorsteps to applaud and cheer. We were there for the nurses and paramedics. We understood how vital our bin men are, how banjaxed we'd be without people willing to stock supermarket shelves or drive all those white vans delivering stuff to our doors. In other words, how reliant we are on people in high-social purpose/low-reward jobs.

The anthropologist David Graeber – who died in 2020 – first shone his merciless light on this reality in 2013. 'In our society,' he wrote, 'there seems a general rule that, the more obviously one's work benefits other people, the less one is likely to be paid for it.'[9]

The Covid pandemic has made this blindingly obvious to us all, hasn't it? The sight of critical care nurses working double shifts for days on end for £30,000 a year made even the most hardhearted City wealth manager blush at the size of the bonuses they draw down for helping rich people minimize their tax liabilities.

'A world without teachers or dock-workers would soon be in trouble,' wrote Graeber, 'and even one without science fiction writers or ska musicians would clearly be a lesser place. It's not entirely clear how humanity would suffer were all private equity CEOs, lobbyists, PR researchers, actuaries, telemarketers, bailiffs or legal consultants to similarly vanish.'

---

[9] David Graeber, *On the Phenomenon of Bullshit Jobs: A Work Rant* strike.coop (August 2013).

Covid made many people hunger for more of a sense of purpose in their work – to do something that is clearly useful for society. The numbers of people approaching me wanting to talk about how they find more meaning and purpose in their work has increased markedly during these times.

I meet all new starters in any business with which I am involved. One young woman who joined our mental health business Togetherall summed it up nicely. 'If you have to sit in your house all day working, you might as well be doing some good for other people, right? You don't want to be at your screen all day just to put money in shareholders' pockets, do you?'

Sustainababble

'It is my fervent hope that we use this crisis as a cata-lyst to rebuild an economy that creates and sustains opportunity for dramatically more people, especially those who have been left behind for too long,' said Jamie Dimon, the billionaire Chairman and CEO of JPMorgan Chase.[10]

Do you believe him or is this just performative marketing spiel?

---

[10] LinkedIn post 19th May 2020.

If the systemic change we need is to happen, then the capital markets must be radically restructured and the role of business reimagined. Even if Caroline's tech business is wildly successful it will only be a small blip on the radar. The bank she left will have to change too if financial inequality is to be properly addressed.

The best known of the sudden rush of corporate leader epiphanies was Larry Fink's. In 2018 he announced to the world in his annual letter to CEOs that social purpose was every bit as important as profit making. Fink runs BlackRock, an enormous investment business with $6 trillion (yes, trillion) under his management, so his awakening matters.

In his January 2021 letter he argued that the Covid-19 pandemic has presented an 'existential crisis' that has 'driven us to confront the global threat of climate change more forcefully and to consider how, like the pandemic, it will alter our lives.'[11]

But is anything really changing? Tariq Fancy is deeply sceptical about the claims of the corporate world that addressing social and environmental issues is not only the right thing to do but also good for business.[12] 'We're running out of time,' he says, 'we can

---

[11] www.blackrock.com/us/individual/2021-larry-fink-ceo-letter

[12] Tariq Fancy, *The Secret Diary of a 'Sustainable Investor'* (August 2021).

no longer afford to answer inconvenient truths with convenient fantasies.' As BlackRock's Chief Investment Officer he was in the belly of the beast, so his cynicism about corporate motives around ESG and impact investing is sobering. He has coined the term 'sustainababble' to describe the verbiage produced by corporate marketing teams to distract from the truth that very little of any substance is changing yet.

Fancy seems like a flaky kumbaya idealist compared to Greta Thunberg whose scathing attacks on corporate obfuscation are well known.

Purpose as performance and product

The burgeoning purpose industry pours out books, podcasts and courses offering advice on how to find meaning in work, business and leadership. LinkedIn is full of newly arrived coaches offering their services to help you find that purpose-aligned job you've always wanted or to start that social enterprise you always said you would but somehow never got around to.

The 'purpose marketplace' is full of poseurs, charlatans, greenwashers and Instagram lifestylers keen for social change so long as it doesn't mean any real change for them or their investments or tax status.

Some of the most narcissistic, hypocritical, unpleasant leaders I have ever met have been those keen to be seen as 'changemakers' and 'social innovators'. Their 'why' is to use social enterprise as a platform for their egos and enjoy the ride on the global social entrepreneur merry-go-round of awards ceremonies and conferences. There is a well-known multi-award-winning smooth operator, for example, who flies the world first class to charm the cash out of the gullible western donors at Skoll and Aspen with stories of miraculous work amongst the poor, returning home to Asia and a big, air-conditioned house and indoor toilets.

I am no saint. I have enjoyed my share of 'look at me saving the world' awards and attention over the years. I have been that man sipping fine wine in fancy hotels in foreign capitals, looking forward to a lovely dinner and being told by a former US president (or some other charlatan trying to wash his record clean) how wonderful I am.

If poverty and injustice could be ended by the hot air generated by the social entrepreneur and sustainability industry in Aspen, Davos or at Oxford's Skoll Forum then they'd be bathing in caviar every day in the slums of Rio and Nairobi.

I chair the board of The Conduit and we describe ourselves as 'a collaborative community of people committed to creating a just, prosperous and sustainable future'. At the heart of our global membership of entrepreneurs, business leaders, investors and non-profit CEOs is a lovely members' club in London's Covent Garden. I see my job there as making sure we do something meaningful and lasting and avoid the very real and ever-present danger of becoming a Taj Mahal of virtue signalling and performance purpose.

The impact delusion?

If you think you have the answers – or some of them – to the world's problems, you need to be very careful about your motives and brutally honest with yourself about the messy mix of personal ambition, emotional neediness, the desire to save, do good, to be known, recognized, rewarded, happy and useful which makes up this 'social entrepreneur' identity. Helder Camara, the Brazilian bishop and champion of the poor, once said, 'The poor are not the raw material of your salvation.'

I was brought up a Catholic and was a diligent altar boy for much of my childhood. From the primary school boy who, for a regular donation, got to adopt an African child and to choose his baptismal name (Paul) to the radical student of liberation theology, my formative years were steeped in it.[13] Indeed I almost become a priest, a missionary to Africa. I rejected it all decades ago but my moral infrastructure still bears the stamp of Rome. I tell my wife that I could be cardinal by now if she hadn't diverted me. She laughs derisively.

In large part because of that upbringing, I have spent all my working life trying to 'make a difference'. But have I and how would I know that I had?

Am I delusional? Despite all my hard work, the hundreds and hundreds of speeches I've given, the millions of pounds raised and invested, the organisations I've created and led, inequality in incomes and health in the UK is worse than in the seventies and the

---

[13] The deeply embedded racism and imperialism of this fund-raising technique by Catholic charities in the 60s struck me hard when in my 30s I found the photo of 'Paul' and my donation records in a shoebox at my mother's home.

climate emergency has shown no sign of responding to my heroic efforts.[14]

Today there is much less chance of a white working-class boy of Irish immigrant stock benefitting from the social mobility in the ways I have. The UK is better in many ways than when I was a kid in the sixties and seventies but so much is worse too, especially the chances of people who start with little overcoming the circumstances of their birth.

Being brutally realistic about all this, what has my purpose-led career amounted to? I have had a great time and people tell me I have had a positive influence in their lives. But would I have been better diving into the City and making money and giving lots of it away? Or doing something really useful such as becoming a nurse or a teacher?

Like optimism, opting for a purpose-driven career path is a choice, made in all our messy humanity and confused and contradictory motives. A choice that, like religious faith, relies on us believing it is the right one even when there is little hard evidence.

Are 'social enterprise' and 'impact investing' at root a spiritual belief system, with their own catechisms and dogmas, high priesthood and miracle workers,

---

[14] According to the Wealth Tax Commission, in 2020 a quarter of all wealth in the UK was owned by just 1% of the population.

sense of purity and sometimes disdainful condescension for the sinners and heretics who cling to the old capitalist gods?

Changing the world, changing nappies

I write about all this not to deter you or depress you. My hope is that the book will encourage you and strengthen your resolve. But your commitment to a purpose-driven job or starting your own social enterprise must be founded on hard realism about the complexity and difficulty of what you are attempting. Knowing why you are pursuing your path of purpose and regularly reviewing your motives and the terms of your engagement are critical to your long-term success – and to your relationships, mental health and well-being.

Caroline is now through the first couple of years of start-up and has raised the money she needs to start really building her business. She has shown amazing resilience and staying power. Nearly three years in, I asked her if she regretted leaving the well-paid corporate job and fancy office in Canary Wharf. 'There have been times, after yet another knock-back, when I have cried, when I've really believed I made a terrible mistake in going down this road and didn't want to admit it to Andrew.'

She argued a lot with her husband during the longer than expected transition from corporate high-flying to socially entrepreneurial self-sufficiency.[15] He saw her commitment to getting her company up and running not as a brave effort to bring innovation to financial services but as a selfish crusade that made her neglect their relationship and threaten their family's security. 'Is it really possible,' Caroline asked me after one particularly toxic row, 'to change the world and be home in time to change the nappies?' These conversations are where noble world-changing visions and the grind of domestic relationships collide (especially for women) and they are what makes mentoring women like Caroline such a privilege.

The world needs many more Carolines. To pursue *your* 'why' you will, like her, need guts, humility, the bloody-minded willingness and ability to bounce back again and again from setbacks, and an ever-deepening knowledge of self that will enable you to thrive over the long haul.

Get yourself a mentor with a state-of-the-art bull-shit detector to help keep you honest. Don't allow your desire for change to swamp your life, take time to recover and be kind to yourself. Honestly, the weight of the world isn't really on your shoulders. Be your

---

[15] It always does take longer!

own fiercest critic, don't take yourself too seriously and *never* believe what is said or written about you, good or bad.

To pursue what you really want will take courage and the willingness to embrace uncertainty and risk. In the second chapter you'll meet Chen, who jumped into the unknown in pursuit of her desire to make a difference and dealt with her fear and the false belief that she isn't a 'proper' businesswoman.

Gloves-off questions

Why is it important to you that you make a positive difference in the world?

What's holding you back from pursuing this purpose?

In what ways has your 'why' changed over the years? Does it need updating?

If your next job was your last job, what would it be?

Chapter Two

On courage, self-belief and taking the plunge

'I will not be regretful on my deathbed that I didn't really try.'

Chen Mao Davies

I met Chen at a social innovation awards ceremony I was MCing in London, in July 2019. I sat in on her pitch sessions and I was fascinated by her story. She had arrived in the UK from China in 2002 speaking little English and with no network at all. She managed to pay her way through university and got her PhD in Computer Graphics. She built a successful career in software design, research and development and for nearly a decade she worked in a world-class studio creating breathtaking visual effects for blockbuster movies. Her team won an Oscar for its work on *Gravity* and *Blade Runner 2049*. Yes, an Oscar.

When she had kids she had a really tough time breastfeeding, especially with latching. Latching refers to how the baby fastens on to the breast. A good latch promotes high milk flow and minimizes nipple discomfort for the mother, whereas a poor latch results in poor milk transfer to the baby and can quickly lead to sore, cracked nipples and even infection. Many women experience intense anxiety and depression as a result of not being able to breastfeed, and babies are deprived of the health and developmental benefits of mothers' milk.

Chen's experience motivated her to create LatchAid, an app to support breastfeeding mothers in those crucial early days after delivery. The app – renamed Anya in 2022 – uses 3D animation technology as well as providing AI-powered, one-to-one support and connecting women to a global community of other new mothers. Her personal experience of the problem she is trying to solve gives her not only profound user insight, but a deep and courageous commitment to women and their well-being.

Chen didn't win the money that night in the City but I was really impressed with her intelligence, passion, commitment and the clear need for Anya in the fast growing 'femtech' market. I gave her my card and said we should have a follow-up coffee, which we did, and I stayed in touch with her on and off for the next year or so, trying to be useful practically and making introductions when and where I could.

In October 2020 one of Chen's colleagues got in touch with me to express her concern that Chen was buckling under the extreme pressure of a demanding full-time job managing a team of software engineers scattered around the world, looking after her family *and* trying to build momentum for her start-up. All of this in the middle of an unprecedented pandemic. I offered my services as a mentor to Chen and we are now working together.

When we reconnected, it was obvious that a punishing toll was being taken on her peace of mind. She wasn't sleeping, she told me, lying awake worrying, feeling she was doing nothing in her life as well as it should be done. The only way through was to be able to commit herself to her start-up or drop it. So, she informed me, she'd handed in her notice and would be leaving her job within weeks. She had money until the end of March – four months away – after which she didn't know what she would do if Anya didn't start to get some real traction – and cash. But she was determined to give it everything she had to make it happen.

'I will not be regretful on my deathbed that I didn't really try.'

Flying or falling?

Chen's courage and commitment stunned me. London is full of 'wantrepreneurs', people who *say* they want to be entrepreneurs, who attend workshop after workshop on innovation and how to set up your own business but who never do it, never take that leap into the unknown which marks out the true innovator from the wannabes and poseurs. Chen's drive to achieve her purpose of reaching as many mothers as possible with state-of-the-art 3D technology outweighed all her financial fears. She had jumped.

She had jumped. If you want to change the world through your own business, the time will come when you need the courage to jump into the unknown, letting go of the certainties we understandably seek to surround ourselves with.

Chen had come to the edge of the cliff, looked down and stepped off. 'How will I know if I'm flying or just falling?' she asked me. Truth is, it is hard to tell when you take the leap in pursuit of your purpose. Courage resides not in jumping when you have all the answers and a Plan B in your back pocket. Courage resides in jumping when there are bloody good reasons not to do so. Family security, predictable income, knowing what you're doing. These are great reasons to turn back and keep the salaried job. No shame in that whatsoever.

Chen had given herself permission, in the most radical way, to really focus on a future shaped by her purpose of helping women. It has been exhilarating and incredibly freeing for her. Not that the worrying and sleepless nights magically went away; bills must still be paid and kids looked after. But when you take that step over the edge, your line of sight on the world changes, possibilities open up, new potential allies can see you, and you certainly find within yourself energy and resilience you didn't know you had.

In the rest of this chapter I'll cover our old friend 'imposter syndrome' and the various sneaky ways it shows up, how it can be turned to your advantage and offer some advice on how to spot when the noise in your own head is stopping you being at your best.

Telling the story

Since that awards gig when we first met, Chen had received some small amounts of short-term project funding from Innovate UK, a public body distributing government cash to encourage innovation. Her contact there had encouraged her to apply for one of the prestigious Women in Innovation Awards.[16]

She had submitted a written application and been shortlisted for interview. With £50,000 at stake as well as the chance for national publicity as a tech role model

---

[16] 'The aim of this competition is to find women with exciting, innovative ideas and ambitious plans that will inspire others. Applicants must be confident, with the support of an award, that they can make a significant contribution to a pressing societal, environmental and/or economic challenge through their innovative project.' www.ukri.org/councils/innovate-uk

for other women, the award would be a big deal at any time for an aspiring entrepreneur. Having handed in her notice, winning one of those coveted places now seemed crushingly important, the final interview a very high stakes roll of the dice.

Chen had been asked to prepare a 10-minute pitch and then submit to a 40-minute grilling from tech and medical professionals convened by Innovate UK. I offered to help her craft her presentation and to put her through her paces by asking her the hardest, most sceptical questions I could think of about the Anya proposition.

Chen sent me her first draft PowerPoint deck. When I read it, what struck me was that she had made herself invisible. She had included lots about software, 3D animation and the negative impacts of poor latching for mother and child, but nothing much at all about Chen. There was no mention of the Oscar! As we spoke about the upcoming pitch it became very clear to me that we needed to focus the mentoring on her self-confidence and bolstering her belief in herself and her phenomenal gifts and bravery.

Chen was gripped by a powerful belief that she was not a 'proper' entrepreneur or businesswoman and everyone would see through her. She would be found out once people interrogated her.

Imposter syndrome

The King's Fund[17] describes 'imposter syndrome' thus:

> 'The term describes a high-achieving individual who struggles to internalise success; who feels fraudulent; and who attributes success to factors such as hard work, charm or luck. Those with 'imposter syndrome' experience a chronic sense of inadequacy.'

Everyone has some variant of this imposter drama except for psychopaths and some FTSE 100 CEOs I have had the misfortune to meet. I have seen it in pretty much everyone I have mentored. There are some systemic causes such as endemic sexism and racism, which obstruct and demotivate women and people of colour. If, like me, you are from a working-class background it can take years to rid yourself of that nagging sense you don't really belong in certain environments, such as boardrooms, with posh people. In the UK class remains a huge barrier to advancement.

Like Chen, I too have doubted that my skills and accomplishments were enough. I often felt going into important meetings that I didn't really deserve to be

---

[17] An English charity that shapes health and social care policy and practice.

there and that one of these days someone would tap me on the shoulder and whisper in my ear, 'I'm so sorry Liam, you've been found out. Please leave and take your pathetic skill set and woefully inadequate experience with you.'

Prison governors, C-Suite executives, unicorn tech founders, bestselling authors, globally successful social entrepreneurs, media CEOs, non-profit super-stars, public sector leaders with huge statutory respon-sibilities – I've met and worked with them all. And all, at times, have allowed their minds to convince them that they are not up to the job, and everyone can see it.

Much of the battle to achieve our purpose happens inside our own head. It consists of dealing with the inner narratives we convince ourselves are telling us something real about our abilities, failings, insecuri-ties. There can of course be very real obstacles in the way but too often the person causing the most obstruc-tion is ourself. The pressures of leadership and entre-preneurship can make those stories we tell ourselves about our lack of worth or right to be in the room as an equal seem all the more real and damaging.

Much of my mentoring work is spent pulling out these inner narratives and helping people fact-check them against actual, you know, reality. This was certainly the case with Chen who, like a lot of software geeks, is an introvert and deeply averse to talking about her undoubted talent and ambition. As a Chinese woman, Chen had been brought up not to push herself forward and not to talk about her own individual contribution.

What Chen saw as her weaknesses – English as a second language, an antipathy towards self-promotion, a disarmingly direct honesty about what she doesn't know – are in fact the very reasons why she *is* a brilliant role model and why, combined with her awesome software and coding abilities and achievements, she could be a real contender for the Innovate UK award.

What panels of judges and audiences of people can smell a mile away is inauthenticity. The work for Chen was to believe that being herself was absolutely enough. You have to be yourself, as Oscar Wilde might have said, because everyone else is taken.

I am a believer in 'if you can't see it, you can't be it' so I had Chen picture herself on the stage getting the Innovate UK award and imagining the women in the audience out in the darkness, beyond the stage lights, being inspired by her and believing that they too could do what she had done. 'Imagine how inspired immigrant women would be,' I told her during one of our conversations. 'All those women who have a great idea for a business, as well as family commitments and a job, seeing you – Chen – up there not because you want to make lots of money but because you want to help women at their most vulnerable.' Those were the women Chen should focus on, not the other contenders whom she feared were smarter, more articulate and 'worthy' than her.

Talking about her Oscar was not laying her open to accusations of showing off but a simple statement of truth about talent and hard work. That part of her story could be communicated in ways that were completely true to Chen's quiet and humble persona.

I have come to see – and encourage my mentees like Chen to see – that this so-called imposter syndrome can be turned to good use. It can mean that we prepare really well. One way of not being found out is to make sure you are bloody well on your game when you need to be. Check and double check. If you're frightened of being found out, make sure you aren't. Presenting skills can be learned and practised, and this is what Chen and I did, working on getting the right blend of tech and market data alongside her personal narrative.

Right up until and throughout the interview Chen felt nervous and, at times, very anxious. 'Sometimes I come awake in the middle of the night and ask myself "what have I done to myself?"' she told me.

Nerves are fine and can be a really good reality check.

On average I have given a speech or lecture to a group of more than 50 people once a month since my mid-twenties. That's more than 500 times I have walked into a room of strangers – often paying good money – to hear me say something interesting and useful. Before each and every one of these events I have felt nerves and often an acute sense of imposter syndrome, especially if I am following someone with a bigger reputation or profile than mine. I still get anxiety dreams the night before a gig about the microphone malfunctioning or people walking out, even though I know my stuff inside out and have learned my stage-craft over the 40 years I have been performing.

When I hear the little voice pipe up about what a pig's ear I am going to make of things, I am grateful. It means I am in the right zone and haven't become complacent. It gives me energy and sharpens my edge.

What's the worst that could happen?

For some of my clients who really do hate 'being on stage', in all senses of that phrase, my advice is to play to their strengths. I suggested to one entrepreneur, who hated giving speeches but had so much to say that was worth hearing about technology and climate change, that when he was invited to participate in a conference he should always insist that his piece was done as a conversation with an interviewer. This has worked really well for him, especially when he sits with a thoughtful and well-informed interlocutor.

One technique I use when I have someone in front of me with a bad case of uncertainty about themselves and their talent, fearful about the upcoming board meeting or business presentation, is to work through with them the possible worst-case scenarios. I make them confront their deepest fears about how useless they are and what is going to go disastrously wrong. In the very act of doing this, the poison is drained from the fangs.

There is a place for positive thinking and imagining the best outcomes; it was really important for Chen to see herself winning the award and being the role model. But there can be a thin line between positive thinking and wishful thinking.

For some people a deeper calm is available by dragging up their most negative visualizations about the future. Exposed to the light of our conscious minds and addressed directly – sometimes to be laughed at – our fears can shrivel and we are better prepared to step into our authority and be at our best.

June asked me to be her mentor when she was appointed to her first CEO role in a very male-dominated business. First-time CEO jobs are particularly challenging as you learn the hard way the leader you really are. All those promises you made to yourself about how you would lead are really put to the fire. The imposter syndrome monkey in the brain can have a field day with the new CEO. This was the case with June. The run-ups to her first few board meetings were fraught times as she would let her mind really get to her. Okay, I said, let the monkey rip. What are your worst fears, list them, don't edit, just let them out. Off she went (as I scribbled them down).

'The board will laugh at my ideas'
'They know I am not right for this job'
'I'm not up to this'
'I'm crap at numbers'
'They know so much more than me'
'They'll think I'm not serious'

On it went, until I had quite the list.

We went through line by line, fact-checking. True or false? 'You're not right for this job and they know it?' False. 'You won a fiercely competitive recruitment process in which all the board were involved.'

'They know so much more than me.' No. 'You were recruited especially because you know more than all of them combined about how digital technology and new business models are disrupting their market.' And so on.

We didn't get the whole list done. June was laughing by the time we'd done the first three points, as she understood that although her fears felt real, they evaporated when exposed to the fresh air of the truth. Don't get complacent, I reminded her, and prepare well, but don't let the things your mind makes up derail you.

In the first six months of her new role we would schedule our sessions for the day before board meetings to make sure she would be in her full personal authority when she walked into the boardroom. This didn't mean that the meetings were easy or that the board of directors didn't hold her to account, but at least she wasn't self-sabotaging by behaving as if the crap her mind made up about her was true. Running a business is hard enough without allowing the imposter syndrome monkey a place at the board table.

It gets better

Dealing with imposter syndrome definitely gets easier with age. You become more confident that you actually do have more experience than everyone else in the room, at least on certain subjects! And, frankly, for me at least, I no longer need or seek the approval of others in the way I did in my twenties and thirties. But there are still traces of it. For me, imposter syndrome is like a toothache that never completely goes away and which flares up unexpectedly from time to time.

Even today – in my sixties – if I am sitting in an unfamiliar boardroom with men I don't know (always men) who display that loud confidence that comes with the expensively acquired private education and upper-middle-class upbringing, I feel a bit edgy before the meeting starts. That little voice pipes up in my brain. *'Liam, they're going to know you don't really belong here, they'll see your working-class roots and second-rate education.'* These days I know not to believe most of what my mind tells me (though the second-rate education piece is correct).[18] Make sure you don't either.

---

[18] Of course imposter syndrome can be crippling for some people and badly undermine confidence and performance. I have referred a few mentees over the years to appropriately trained mental health practitioners.

You are certainly not alone. 'Remember,' counsels Oliver Burkeman, 'the reason you can't hear other people's inner monologues of self-doubt isn't that they don't have them. It's that you only have access to your own mind.'[19] Acknowledging that you feel like an imposter at times is an important first step to finding your confidence. If you are in a leadership position, being honest about it to yourself at least might help with your empathy with those for whom you are responsible. Knowing that they will be dealing with their own mental monkeys could make you a better boss.

'I'm a fraud' is not the only way that imposter syndrome can show up, though. Here are some other things to be on the lookout for.

Comparing yourself unfavourably with others

A big cog in my anxiety generator over the years has been the habit of comparing myself with others whom I perceive to be more successful, creative, happier, productive, famous. Try not to do this. Everyone's success is unique. You never know the full story of their struggles, mistakes and huge strokes of luck. The

---

[19] Oliver Burkeman is a writer and broadcaster and author of the rather splendidly titled *The Antidote: Happiness for People Who Can't Stand Positive Thinking* (2012). The quote used here is from *The Guardian* 4th September 2020.

lives and successes of others are always a lot messier and more contingent than you imagine.

There are of course many people who really are better looking, richer, more creative, who are having a bigger more positive impact in the world than I am, and they may be happier than me, too. Fair play to them. Their existence and success say nothing about me or my abilities. 'Insist on yourself,' said Ralph Waldo Emerson. 'Never imitate.'

Overly focussing on the negative

One of my mentees is a congenital underminer of good news or positive feedback about his performance. If he scored the winning goal at the World Cup he'd beat himself up for not scoring a hat trick. We have worked on it a lot as we deal with this internal *'I'm not really good enough am I?'* melodrama.

Colin worked for a global manufacturer, reporting to a very demanding CEO who prided himself on not suffering fools gladly. We worked for weeks to prepare him for a make-or-break presentation to the boss on an important part of the company's future sustainability strategy. It was a key moment in Colin's ambition to really make a positive difference to the world through the business.

On the day of the pitch, I waited for as long as I could before getting in touch to find out how it went. At 8pm I texted him:

'Marks out of 10?'
'3 or 4.'
'Shit. What happened?'
'Took me apart on some of the numbers.'
'Bugger.'
'Yeah, it was a nightmare.'
'So you didn't get the plan agreed?'
'Yes.'
'Yes you didn't get plan agreed??'
'Yes – plan agreed.'
'FFS Colin. So it's really 9/10??!!'
☺

I'm not saying don't pay adequate attention to the negatives and I don't recommend a Pollyanna approach to leadership. If you want to change the world then regular ruthless honesty about where you might be missing the mark or underachieving is essential. When you've messed up, of course, you must try and learn from it and not do it again. But get out of the habit of always going to the negative first and obsessing over it. It is a healthy habit to start meetings with some good news and I encourage my clients to bring to our sessions something great that has happened since we last met, before we get into the psychodramas!

So, what about Chen?

Well, reader, she won the award and was announced as one of Innovate UK's Women in Innovation in March 2021!

She was informed about the win on a Friday – the very day she was leaving her salaried job! You couldn't make it up, could you? Perhaps the story of her life will be made into an Oscar-winning movie one day.

Much hard work lies ahead as Chen builds out the business and seeks investors. She is making good progress but there is no guarantee of success. But she has confronted her fears about herself and her abilities and found the words to tell her story authentically. She has stepped into the role of purpose-driven leader and businesswoman with confidence and integrity – and she believes it.

Let's now move on to how best to synch *what* you want to do with *how* and *where* you'll do it. Are you in the right place to make the difference you want?

Gloves-off questions

If you are not doing what you really want to – start that business, get that new job – what is *really* holding you back?

June refuses to give the mind monkeys a seat at her board table. How much of what you think is holding you back is in your head, fears your mind has made up?

Chapter Three

Purpose and platform

Cameras flash, champagne bottles pop, glasses tinkle.

It's 2007 and I'm standing on a stage in a London Bridge nightclub heaving with people. In front of me it's wall-to-wall celebrities, government ministers, media and creative types and anyone who's anyone in the London restaurant scene.

Celebrity chef Jamie Oliver has just jumped jack-in-the-box style from a huge mock cake to tumultuous laughter and applause. The stage is packed with young people in their chefs' whites, alumni of the Fifteen apprenticeship programme. We're all here to celebrate the fifth birthday of the business and our brilliant ecosystem of cooks, waiters, sommeliers, suppliers, farmers, educators, funders and sponsors.

This should be one of the highlights of my career but I feel awful and I just don't want to be there. I'm on autopilot, running on empty, grinning broadly, doing my schtick as the funny, in-control, authority-figure CEO, the foil to Jamie's cool big brother to the youngsters.

I look like I'm having a great time. But I'm hating it.

Four years earlier, Jamie persuaded me to leave Liverpool and come to London to sort out the Fifteen business and create a viable longer-term strategy for a social enterprise with a global profile.

I was attracted by the challenge of trying my hand in a new industry and the excitement of a global platform to promote my brand of purpose-driven business. It was a great big boost to my ego and the money was pretty good too.

Fifteen was an upmarket restaurant opened as part of a reality TV show in 2002 called *Jamie's Kitchen*. Named for the first 15 young people recruited to the chef apprenticeship scheme, the place was incredibly popular and people travelled from all over the world to dine with us and feel part of Jamie's mission. The air in the kitchen was thick with the pungent aroma of freshly made pasta and the sweat, ambition and insecurities of young people.

I loved the purpose at the heart of the venture. We provided potentially life-changing opportunities for our young apprentices recruited from London's prisons and homeless hostels.

We offered troubled young people a different sort of gang. Not one that would abuse or kill them but one that opened up the world to them. We offered purpose and a sense of belonging as well as a set of practical skills in high demand in every city of the world, in a profession made cool by chefs like Jamie. Jamie's commitment was never in doubt and he was a genuine inspiration to the apprentices. His energy and drive were phenomenal, and I learned a lot from him.

I travelled a lot to promote the brand and oversaw the franchising of the concept in Amsterdam, Cornwall and Melbourne. We inspired copycat social enterprise restaurants all over the world, from Saigon to Sao Paolo.

Invitations came in daily to speak at conferences all over the world; the media were always willing to cover us, celebrities were keen to be associated with Jamie and the young people. City leaders - and sometimes heads of state - from all over the globe were lobbying us to open a Fifteen in their countries. But whilst the purpose of Fifteen was very much in line with my desire to do useful and meaningful work, to have a job which made a real difference in the lives of others, the platform on which I was pursuing that purpose increasingly was not the right place for me. Standing on that stage in London Bridge, I realized I had to leave. Emotionally and psychologically, I badly mishandled my transition out. All my own fault. I should have got myself a coach or mentor to help me prepare mentally and emotionally for the shocks inherent in such a change of role and identity. I didn't want to share all my fears and anxieties with my wife, Maggie. I felt like it was burdening her. And if I'm being totally honest with you, it felt like a weakness to own up to the fears I had about walking away from that CEO role, which, it would turn out, was my last one in someone else's business.

Fifteen went on to support many more young people for over a decade and Jamie's social mission around food and inequality continues to this day.

Tricky transitions

More than fifteen years later, this alignment of personal purpose with the right platform is fundamental to most of the work I do with my mentees – whether they are in senior corporate roles, are business founders or CEOs of non-profits.[20] The work is often done in

---

[20] I am grateful to Dr Aravind Srinivisan for many conversations about purpose and platform. He taught me a lot.

that tricky time of transition when people feel it's time to move on because purpose and platform are out of synch.

Lately, there are a lot of people who feel that misalignment dragging them down. I receive regular LinkedIn messages that start with some variation of 'Covid really forced me to think about what I want to do with my life...'.

Anxiety, boredom, frustration, irritability or underperformance can all be signs that your purpose and platform are out of whack. Happiness (or at least satisfaction) happens when your purpose – how you want to spend your talent and time to make a difference in the world – is aligned with your platform – the organisational model you operate within and the culture and people in and around it.

If you want to put social purpose, making a lasting difference, at the heart of your leadership and working life, then a regular review of the platform you are choosing to make that purpose real is a must. It amazes me how many people don't do this work and unconsciously accommodate themselves to the place they are and the people they are with – even when that requires trimming and compromises that eventually undermine effectiveness, self-belief and peace of mind.

In the rest of the chapter I will go deeper into 'purpose and platform' through the experiences of three people I have mentored and draw again from my own career, this time when I reset my life and work after a 10-year business partnership.

Let me now introduce you to the first of these people who turned to me for advice and support when the disruption created by the clash of purpose and platform became something he just had to deal with.

'What will I do for the next 10 years?'

Gerald stopped me as I was walking out of a room where I had just given a presentation about mentoring. 'I think we need to talk', he said.

Before our meeting two weeks later, I did some online research. Now in his late forties, he had had, by any measure, a spectacularly successful career. He was a prominent mover and shaker amongst London's digital glitterati and anyone he didn't know in private equity or venture capital probably wasn't worth knowing.

In his mid-thirties he had sold one of his businesses to a multinational, the first of a series of smart moves from which he had done very well. As a serial entrepreneur, angel investor, board member, chairman, sought-after speaker, philanthropist, he had received an MBE for services to the digital economy.

Once he had told me about his wife and kids, I asked Gerald to describe his professional life. In these first sessions I like to draw a mind map of clients' responsibilities and accountabilities to help me get a sense of the shape and rhythm of their working lives. He started talking, I started scribbling. I gave up after four pages. As I drew, he remembered more and more. 'Oh yeah, I'm on the board of So and So. I invested there five years ago. Oh, and I'm a trustee at Such and Such charity.'

Eventually, I put the pen down. 'So, what do you want to talk about,' I asked.

'I feel anxious and restless and I'm getting into lots of stupid scraps with partners and investors. How do I get less chippy and irritable with people? I'm not enjoying any of it much. I can be a bit of a dickhead.'

The complicated and messy diagram of his professional life was a pretty accurate depiction of where he was at. He had lost focus and was all over the place – literally running from meeting to meeting around central London with no clear sense of direction about why. He was busy being busy. It was clear he had made some impulsive decisions that he now regretted. He'd lost himself and it was frustrating him. He was taking that frustration out on people by being unreasonable and prone to flying off the handle.

'How do you feel about being nearly 50?' I asked.

'It's been worrying me, to be honest. What will I do for the next 10 years?'

Fifty is a tricky one for many people. It certainly was for me; 40 and 60 were breezes in comparison. At 50, you can't pretend you're young anymore but you're not *that* old and you probably have at least 20 maybe 30 years of productive life left in you. What are you going to do to fill it meaningfully – especially if most of your biggest successes came, as Gerald's did, much earlier in your career?

For Gerald, the public platform of 'The Entrepreneur Who Made It in His Thirties' was outdated; continuing to occupy it was making him increasingly uncomfortable and he was taking it out on the people around him. He wasn't happy in his skin and he needed to find a new one, to very consciously choose the identity he wanted in his fifties.

By the end of that first two-hour session we had reframed Gerald's issue. It wasn't about his grumpy unreasonableness: that was just the visible part of the problem, the symptom. He had lost sight of his purpose over the last couple of years and consequently, Gerald's self-confidence had drained from him. He was getting depressed.

At root it was about renewing that purpose and then finding the right platform for him to deploy his considerable talents and resources as he passed the Big

Five-Oh. We agreed that the goal of our mentoring work was to come up with a plan that answered the question: 'How do I make my fifties the best decade yet?'

As an outsider who pays very close attention, one of the great gifts a mentor can bring is a clear-eyed view of what your problem really is. In my experience the issue a potential client presents is often not what's really bothering them. In the middle of your own life, it is very hard not to catch a bad case of Woods and Trees Syndrome. Gerald's case was acute.

Resetting

Gerald's platform – his portfolio of investments, non-exec directorships – was no longer nourishing his purpose. Indeed he could no longer see clearly what his purpose was and this was doing his head in. His messy, incoherent platform was crumbling beneath him and his confidence was crashing.

When the misalignment is as serious as Gerald's, a major reset is required. For him the trigger was his approaching 50th birthday. (Maybe that's what a mid-life crisis is – the sudden awareness of the lack of alignment between purpose and platform.) The reset trigger can be a falling-out with a business partner, the arrival of a new boss you can't stand, a lack of challenge or limited scale of impact. It will be different for everyone.

Over our 10 hours of mentoring, Gerald investigated what he would need to do short term and longer term to get to where he wanted to be. How could he construct a new platform, one on which he could happily stand into his sixth decade?

We started by decluttering his life, going through the lists of his commitments and asking, 'Do you want to take this into your fifties or do you want to leave it behind?' In some instances, walking away meant taking a financial hit but he could see that the longer-term benefits of peace of mind and energy would be well worth it.

He is a very bright guy who acts quickly once he's made up his mind. He motored through his list of commitments using these three criteria:

1. Don't like doing it, can't wait to be rid of it and I can do that quickly by just resigning.
2. Don't like doing it but have to stay involved for now, either for financial or reputational reasons.
3. Love doing it, this is coming into my fifties with me.

Over the course of our six months together we hacked back his roles and responsibilities. I drew another map at our last meeting. It fitted on one page and felt as if it laid out a coherent terrain in which he could find himself again.

Gerald was lucky, he is not reliant on a salary and he only had to make decisions for himself. Resetting can be very fraught and difficult if you are in business with someone else and your choices have serious implications for others, as was the case with the second mentee I want to introduce to you now.

'I feel like a stranger in my own company'

I first met Kiran in spring 2018, introduced by a mutual friend. Kiran was then the co-owner of a business she founded with a university mate when they were in their early thirties. The business was a roaring, award-winning success, growing rapidly, leaving competitors in its wake and delighting investors.

But in our first session over lunch Kiran told me how unhappy she was and how anxious about the increasing antagonism with her business partner. Meetings were getting fraught, communications were breaking down, seeing each other socially had stopped, the fun had gone, and the employees knew it. 'I find myself sitting in a board meeting talking about the HR issues we have amongst our staff. This isn't what I had in mind at all when we started up. I just don't like being around there some days. I feel like a stranger in my own company.'

The more we spoke, and the trust grew between us, the clearer it became that this was not just a case of two people growing apart under the pressures of a fast-growing business. The relationship breakdown was a symptom of something much deeper. Kiran's purpose and the platform of her business were no longer aligned, and she was struggling to come to terms with that reality.

One night in an email exchange about yet another internal meeting which had gone wrong, I asked her: 'What do you really want?'

In the wee hours back came her long and passionate reply, which included these two lists:

What do I want?
I want to be proud of what I am doing
I want to be involved in big projects
I want autonomy in what I do. I don't want to be fearful of my business partner or feel constrained by a way of doing things that I don't agree with.
I want to be happy when I'm with my family
I want to have fun

Why will I succeed?
I am hugely resilient
I have amazing energy, knowledge and
understanding
I know big financing
I am entrepreneurial
I have big ideas
I am a good person, and a new type of leader

Have you ever written out similar lists of what you really want and why you've got what it takes to get it? Try it.

Kiran seemed to be moving towards the exit, saying that she wanted to leave and start another business on her own. But this is a high-risk route to take. Her present company was already making a big difference and, I asked her, was she just allowing a bad patch and cranky relationships to obscure the big picture that this business was in fact the platform from which she could achieve her very ambitious purpose-related goals? After all, running a business of any size requires having to do some boring and energy-sapping things with people you would rather not have to deal with on a regular basis.

If you've ever had to go through the long days of due diligence to land investment, or led on a merger, or had to wrestle with a difficult board, or manage your way through a cash crunch, you know that sometimes you just have to suck it up and get the work done. Unglamorous, dull, hard yards work. You can't change the world without a great deal of that. Shit happens in leadership, get over it. Or as a head chef I once worked with would shout at his weary kitchen brigade at 9.30pm on a busy Friday night, 'Come on! Head down, arse up, keep chopping!'

Was Kiran's problem that her inexperience was telling and she just needed to understand the hard realities of leadership – especially with a partner who relished being in charge and commanding a fast-growing army of employees? Did she need to grow a thicker skin, get her arse up and keep chopping?

From common ground to minefield

I suggested that Kiran owed it to herself and her co-founder partner to make every effort to repair and reset their relationship. They retained a coach to facilitate the conversations, but after a couple of sessions it was clear they were going nowhere. Kiran was shocked to discover that the common ground between them had all but disappeared and what was left had become a minefield of unexpressed resentments and misunderstandings about motives and intentions. Long gone were the exciting days of start-up, the 'in it together, one for all and all for one', 'us against the world' passion and commitment.

A temporary fix was agreed but it seemed to me that the writing was on the wall in huge red letters and it read 'EXIT'. In my heart of hearts, I knew Kiran would be leaving. She would really come alive describing what she might do when she was free of her present situation. She began more and more to focus on that different future and I could see the entrepreneur light come back on, bright and strong.

As Kiran's mentor, I was very careful not to use the undoubted influence I have with her to push her in one direction or another. If you choose to make a platform change as significant as the one that Kiran seemed to be leaning towards, it must be 100% *your* choice. You must be able to get everything you have behind it. Of course, I was not the only person Kiran was talking to about all of this. Her husband, parents, friends all had a point of view.

At this point in anyone's platform transition, confusion and anxiety are common and this was the case with Kiran. She was worried that she was missing something and that she might deeply regret leaving the business she had done so much to build. She was scared.

I suggested that we get out of the city and into the countryside for a long walk. I often take clients for 'walkie talkies' in the Chiltern hills when there's an important conversation needing to be had. The extended time together, the fresh air, the lack of distractions (phones left in cars), seem to really help us get to the bottom of things. (For the lazy mentor there are many readily handy metaphors about 'paths to take', 'wood for the trees', 'changing seasons' and 'struggling uphill'.)

I told her I was going to really push her on her resolve to exit. Playing devil's advocate, I would try as hard as I could to persuade her that leaving was the wrong decision. One of the best ways to think through and sharpen – or abandon – your position or plan of action is to be confronted by the best case against it.

I had diligently prepared my devil's advocate case and I enthusiastically went for it. After all, I did know Kiran really well, and the strengths and possibilities of her business. But she had prepped well too, and she had robust and deeply thoughtful answers to all my best arguments. At the end of our four-hour hike we both had the strong sense that she had reached clarity about her future.

And so it proved. The focus of our next conversations changed from, *'How do you develop the tools to cope inside this business you have created?'* to *'How do you leave well and create a new platform for yourself to pursue your best life and business purposes?'*

She set a date by which she wanted to be out of the business and we drew a map of the conversations she needed to have with those who would be affected by her reset. These included her husband, co-founder, principal investors and board directors.

Once her reset plan was made, her anxiety levels dropped. There were still some tough meetings ahead and the money discussions were bruising (they usually are). She missed her deadline by a couple of months but once she got the clarity that her task was to create another platform to pursue her purpose, she was more than halfway there.

As I write this, Kiran is raising investment for her next business and she is loving it. She is also very clear about the sort of culture she wants to create and is explicit about this with the leadership team she is recruiting.

Many business partnerships end very badly because co-founders are too focussed on the business and do not give anywhere near enough attention to having honest conversations about their relationships and the culture they allow to be created.

Starting and building a business changes you, and if co-founders don't develop and sustain the habit of talking regularly and honestly about what is going on in their minds and hearts, they will grow apart. The risk of breakdown mounts. Avoid the difficult conversations about roles, money, ego, authority and power at your peril because, if you do, relationships will drift blindly into dysfunction and the risk of a messy and painful separation increases.

What is the conversation you would least like to have with your boss or business partner, the one that makes you feel anxious and you always find reasons to avoid? That is the very one you should be having. And you know it.

What am I doing here?

In advising Kiran, I was able to draw on my own experience of decoupling from business partners.

In 2007, after I tumbled out of Jamie World, I co-founded Wavelength with two friends.[21] We challenged senior leaders to 'change the world for the better through business'. We ran leadership courses, conferences, masterclasses and study tours for leaders from the corporate, public and non-profit sectors, operating a cross-subsidy business model to enable the 'non-profits' to be in the same room, as peers, with their richer counterparts from big business.

---

[21] www.wavelengthleadership.com

For six or seven years Wavelength was the perfect platform for me. I travelled all over the world. The business was paid handsomely for me to run events and give speeches about leadership, innovation and social change. I felt I was making a real difference and we helped shape some great innovations such as the UK's first impact investment fund, which channelled tens of millions of pounds into purpose-led businesses in healthcare, housing and youth empowerment.[22]

The business did really well and we had a client list to die for. The money was great and I got to meet lots of very cool people doing interesting things.

Wavelength was my 'passion cross-subsidy platform', the highly paid work with the corporate C-Suites enabling me to do what I really loved doing – working with the social entrepreneurs, social innovators and changemakers (who had no money!). I really felt that I was making a lasting difference. I loved it.

But as the years passed, I found myself resenting the time spent listening to corporate clients on huge salaries trying to work out how they could change their company's culture or find their place in the digital revolution. Hosting a session at one of the tech companies in Silicon Valley, listening to a senior executive

---

[22] Impact Ventures UK, a 10-year capital growth fund managed by Lightrock.

dodging a question about why the company doesn't pay its fair share of tax, I thought: 'What am I doing here? I've had enough of this.'

I was in my mid-fifties and had recently become a grandfather, which had made me really think about my place in the universe (as a recovering Catholic I am prone to spasms of morose metaphysical introspection as, reader, you've no doubt noticed).

On my flight back to London, sipping a Bloody Mary and looking wistfully out of the window, I admitted to myself that I wanted to leave the business and focus solely on the stuff I wanted to do.

For a few weeks I sat with my growing unease and anxiety, biting my lip in meetings, lacking the courage to face the angry pushback I feared would come from my partners. My premature exit, after all, would have major implications for them.

Coming home late one night on the train from a work gig I decided the time had come. I drew this diagram and wrote out two lists on my phone.

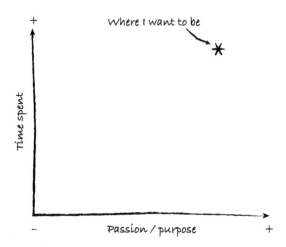

List one: What I don't want to do any more…

1. I don't want to have to compromise with business partners, even when it is the right thing to do.
2. I don't want to listen ever again to senior leaders talking about the necessity of change but doing everything in their power not to make any.
3. I don't want to ever bite my tongue for fear of losing business.
4. I don't want to spend a minute longer with tedious Alpha males with egos way bigger than their talent who think they know all the answers.

5. I don't want to go to Silicon Valley ever again and put up with rich men talking about a tech utopia in which they have no accountability, have all the money and pay no tax.

6. I don't want to hear the sound of my own voice trotting out the same shtick every sales cycle. No more Bullshit Bingo of senior leadership, 'going forward', 'headwinds', 'disruptive innovation', 'low hanging fruit', 'blah blah blah'.

LEADERSHIP BS

LINGO **BINGO** CARD

Going Forward	Pivot	The People Piece	RESULTS DRIVEN
WIN/ WIN	REACH OUT	CIRCLE BACK	DEEP DIVE
Walk the Walk	Your Favourite Bullshit Term HERE	SYNERGIES	Value Added
HEADWINDS	Low Hanging Fruit	CADENCE	We're on a Journey

You don't need to be an occupational therapist or psychiatrist to discern my urgent need to move on and reset!

List two: What I love doing and want to do more of...

1. Being around changemakers and entrepreneurs building something new and useful.
2. Using my experience and networks to enable others to go further, faster.
3. Mobilising capital and talent to build purpose-driven businesses.
4. Having my voice heard in the world and inspiring the young.

As I write these words, nearly five years after resetting it all, I'm pleased to report that this list sums up pretty well what I am now doing with my life.

In the end, my partners were perfectly reasonable and we ended our business partnership well. Wavelength continues to thrive without me and I daresay my co-founders' lives are much less complicated without me there asking awkward questions.

Write out your own lists. Perhaps your first list – what you don't want to do any more – is very short, and the list of what you love doing aligns with the work you do. If so, all power to you. If not, and you discover that what you are doing now does not line up with what you would love to be spending your time doing, perhaps a reset is on the cards for you.

However, a reset doesn't necessarily mean leaving the organisation you are with now. Perhaps negotiating a new role is the answer, as it was for the third and final mentee I want to introduce to you in this chapter.

'I want to smell oil again, Liam'

Willem was a senior director at a global aerospace business who asked me for advice about his future. He had joined 20 years ago from university as an engineer, and loved getting his hands dirty building aircraft engines. As he rose up the corporate ladder he had moved further and further away from the factory floor. 'I'm now responsible for 10,000 people all over the world and I never even get to smell the oil let alone go home covered in it. I want to smell oil again, Liam!'

He was considering resigning but I suggested he go to the board and tell them honestly how he was feeling. My hunch was that they would not want to lose someone with his experience and commitment to a company he loved. 'You're thinking of leaving anyway. What have you got to lose?' I asked him.

And so it was. The board were shocked to hear that one of their best performers and most loyal and long-serving leaders was considering quitting. They asked him what he wanted and he told them straight. A couple of months later Willem transferred to another leadership role where he was dealing directly with designers and engineers. He took a bit of a pay cut but loved the new job, regaining a lot of the enthusiasm that had motivated him as a graduate trainee.

Willem stayed in the business for another seven years, leaving at 50 to start his own renewable energy business. Today he is, as they say in Berlin, *sehr glücklich*.

Resetting at any stage of life is not easy and you have to put the time in. But you will feel a profound sense of relief that you are taking yourself seriously and doing some structured, deep work on what you want in life and how you can ensure that the best lies ahead of you.

To mark the end of our time together and to help him stick to the commitments he had made, I knocked up this sticker for Gerald to put on his fridge.

My 50's : The Best Decade Yet

I will be happy in mind and body, making time to enjoy and support my family, aspire to be a great husband and engage in work which excites and fulfils me.

I will make a lasting and important impact in the world whilst fully true to who I am.

Outside the family and farm, I will only do work which plays to my strengths and passions, where I can:

Be a connector
Bring an edge
Provide encouragement
Enable through technology
Be part of a team where I can teach and learn

I will never again put myself in positions where I am carrying the load alone and I will never again jump off the cliff without looking.

What would be on your fridge? How would you describe your purpose and, having got clear about that, are you on the right platform?

So, you've done some work on your motivations, you know why you want to change the world, you've taken the plunge and started your own business, social enterprise or left one job to join another organisation which better suits your purpose. Now you've got to the position of leadership you want. But how are you going to use that authority? That's what we'll deal with in the next chapter.

Gloves-off questions

Are your purpose and platform in synch?

Sit somewhere nice and quiet and write out these two lists, being as honest with yourself as possible.

List one: What I don't want to do any more...
List two: What I love doing and want to do more of...

If you are considering a reset in your work these simple questions may be helpful to you.[1]

What do you want to do?
Why is it important to you? How will you define and measure success? What are the critical conditions for achieving it?

Where are you now?
What is your current reality – honestly? What can you leverage? What assets and networks can you call on to get you where you want to be? Where are the biggest gaps?

What next?
Define what needs to happen now. What will have the biggest impact? What are the key steps and when will you take them?

---

[1] My thanks to my friends at lspleadership.com

Chapter Four

Authority and agency

For many of the people I work with it is quite a shock to get to a leadership position and find it is not what they were expecting. This was vividly brought home to me by this message emailed to me at the end of a first-time CEO's first week on the job.

> 'Jesus, Liam. I didn't expect it to be so hard. It's a real shock to me to find out I don't know how to use my authority. My big vision for this business gets mugged every day I go in. I want to change the world and I'm mired in "he said, she said" playground stuff. Does everyone lie to the CEO?'

Isabelle worked for 20 years in a global financial services business, with relentless sales targets and constant international travel. Her experience was that so much energy at C-Suite level is misdirected.

'None of us at that level were doing what we knew we really should be doing. Your focus is on surviving the organisation, preparing for the next board meeting or getting through that next presentation to the exco.'

She had a big budget, reported direct to the CEO and still she flew around the world, exhausted, to chair meetings on multiple change projects that never quite came to fruition. It slowly dawned on her that her ability to effect lasting change was really small. 'Agency as a leader in a big business is vastly over-stated,' she told me.

Paul took over a charity for the homeless, providing shelter and care for some of London's most damaged and challenging rough sleepers. He had expected to be spending most of his time engineering radical new approaches to mental health and housing. But no. He found himself dealing with arsey, underperforming staff who had been allowed to get away with murder by his predecessor. 'I would rather deal with a rough sleeper on crack coming at me with a chair than sit in another grievance meeting with that sanctimonious bastard who runs our operations.' Our sessions were enjoyably feisty.

When not wading through HR treacle up to his chest and dealing with the psychodramas of non-profit entitlement, Paul had to learn to cope with a panicky interfering chairman who really believed that 30 years in a bank qualified him as an expert in all aspects of social policy and, indeed, the human condition. 'I thought as a CEO I would be in charge,' Paul told me at one of our first sessions in a Euston pub, 'but I feel like the most powerless person in the place.'

So, now what?

Exercising the authority and power a leadership position should confer is a big issue with all those I mentor. Getting to the exco table or the CEO's office is one thing, working out how to inhabit the role effectively is quite another. You may have arrived in a role where you *should* be able to make a difference, but working out *how* you do that is something else again.

Much of my mentoring work is about helping people understand the leader they want to be, and to exercise authority in ways which are true to their values and get the job done.

In large organisations in any sector, getting anything meaningful done is really difficult because of complex and long-embedded cultural and behavioural norms. Changing those cultures is incredibly difficult.

If you're trying to do that at the same time as learning how to lead and working out what sort of leader you want to be, well, good luck with that!

This chapter is written to help you get straight about how you will lead and the work you need to do to get to that clarity. I have also included a big reminder that grandiose theories and aspirations about your leadership are worthless if you don't ensure that the basics of running your organisation are sorted out.

John's story

Agency was at the heart of the mentoring relationship I had with John, who had risen fast in the ranks of a well-known company championed by a CEO who was in a great hurry to make his mark on the business.

Coming out of his annual appraisal, the company offered to pay for a mentor, which is where I came in. This was the brief John and I settled on:

- How do I lead a group of highly intelligent, really talented, opinionated peers whose default setting is to look for faults and weaknesses?
- I need to work on my leadership presence, how I come over, how I give others the confidence to come with me.

John was only in his mid-thirties when he arrived at the exco table, a good 10 years younger than everyone else in the team. He is a super intelligent strategic thinker and an introvert, given to listening and processing much more than talking, let alone competitive talking with pushy extroverts.

His starting position was, 'Well, if I have nothing worth saying I will stay quiet.' I pointed out that his colleagues, talented though they undoubtedly were, could probably not read minds and were thus likely to interpret his silence as evidence of his unsuit-ability to be in the room since he had nothing of worth to impart.

My concern was that his CEO – a very char-ismatic guy untroubled by self-doubt who only wanted the best for John – was trying to fit John into a specific mould of what leadership behaviour looks like. In other words, he was trying to make John lead like he does.

In our first sessions we worked on what type of leader John wanted to be. If he was being at his best – and how he wanted to be – how would others describe what it was like to experience his leadership?

We then talked about what practical steps he could take to move towards that place. Some of this was very tactical – looking at agendas for key upcoming meetings and deciding where John could intervene to best effect.

If he was chairing the meeting, then we would work on his opening remarks and techniques for running the session that would enable as many people as possible to play, but would clearly signal his authority. We worked together on the script he would use to begin the meeting so that it would have the pace and focus he brought into the room.

In the early days of this work, John was nervous about trying out new techniques so I would make myself available on the phone an hour before key meetings to coach him into the mindset of being fully in his authority.

A longer-term strategy was strengthening and, where necessary, creating relationships with his peers in the leadership team. He needed each member of the group to understand more about him, his talent and aspirations, and how he could support them, and that is just not possible to create in a time-pressurized meeting when everyone is inevitably jockeying for attention and airtime.

His colleagues – all very talented and at the top of their games – didn't stop being like a bag of ferrets at meetings but John's presence in the mix improved, and feedback from his very detailed 360-degree annual appraisal provided the evidence that he had risen in their estimation. He was now seen as being in the room with them on his merits, not as the protégé of the CEO.

One tricky issue was to reset the relationship between John and his CEO, who had strongly championed his rise up the hierarchy. The relationship had been invaluable but we agreed it was very father/son and that this needed to be recast in the interests of both. John showed considerable bravery in taking this on. Your CEO can help make or break your career and when that person is a leading figure in the wider industry, it is critical to get the relationship right to ensure mutual benefit.

I suggested to John that he take the CEO out of the office to discuss how their relationship might evolve. This not only levelled the field a bit, it also ensured that the meeting was less likely to be bumped or interrupted. The practicalities around such important career conversations are important. So think them through.

I often propose to those I mentor, when they have to have a critical conversation, that they frame it as part of their mentoring work. 'My mentor asked me a great question about the dynamics of how you and I work together...'

In John's case, the business was funding my mentoring so it was easier to have these conversations.

Indeed at the end of the first year, the CEO asked to see us both to discuss progress and whether the business was getting value for money.

I had a lot of respect for the CEO so didn't bullshit him by doing anything other than being direct about parts of his relationship with John which we thought needed to change. It was at times a spiky meeting but it ended very positively, most importantly, for John.

The final phase of our mentoring was to discuss what was next for John. He decided to leave, having concluded that he'd got as far as he could there and that it was time to continue developing his leadership somewhere else.

He had broken the co-dependency with a CEO who had put his time and the company's money into creating space for John to work on his agency and presence as a leader in a high-performing team – and, unusually, was willing to listen to feedback about their relationship which he really didn't want to hear. John will have much to be grateful for to that man, as he goes on to great things in his career.

Choose and practise

You can choose the behaviours you want to develop as a leader. In part this will be decided by your person-ality type and previous experiences but there is much that can be consciously worked on and deepened. Once chosen, the job is to practise, practise, practise until it becomes your practice as leader.

One of the leaders I greatly admire is Sue Campbell, who is the UK Football Association's director of women's football and was previously, for 10 years, chair of UK Sport. Sue is widely credited with transforming the infrastructure around UK elite sport that drove the profound culture and expectation changes that set the nation up for its remarkable successes at London 2012 and on to Rio 2016 and Tokyo 2020. She also played a critical role in the backroom and board transformation of the culture around elite women's football which led to the joyous success of the Lionesses at Euro 2022.

Like many great leaders she has the ability to make things simple and to communicate them clearly. When she takes over a leadership role she asks the people who work for her three questions:

'What do you?'
'What could you do?'
'What's stopping you?'

The first question helps her really understand what it is her team are doing with their time and energies. Don't assume you know what your colleagues and peers are doing, really get to the heart of it and understand how much of their time and talent – and the organisation's resources – are being misdirected and wasted. If you are new to a leadership role this is critical for you to grasp quickly.

The second question – 'What could you do if there were no constraints?' – gives people permission to get excited about the possibilities of their work, perhaps to recover the enthusiasm they first had when they took up their roles. If you don't understand the motivations of your team then you'll not get the most from them. This is especially important in an impact-driven business where alignment of values and purpose are core to success at all levels.

Sue's third question – 'What's stopping you from achieving as much as you can and want to?' – helps to uncover inefficiencies, resentments, system blockages and all the other stuff which builds up in any organisation and undermines focus and delivery.

Having asked her three questions, Sue then sees her core leadership job as removing the barriers which get in the way of people being at their best and collaborating for the common good.

Leadership is messy, inevitably so since we have no choice but to deal with other human beings – as colleagues, bosses, customers, investors – with all our flaws, complexities, contradictions and dramas. I have spent decades looking for a profitable business with no employees or customers. If you know of one, please introduce me! In a purpose-driven business, people are not just there for the money, they come with all sorts of motivations. Leading them can be tricky, so knowing who you are as a leader and how you want to exercise your authority is even more important. If you don't do the work, prepare for trouble.

Brilliant basics, magic touches: a reminder

So, good leaders will do the work of understanding their motivations and blind spots, develop their resilience and grit, work on their storytelling and culture-building skills, and build great networks across and outside the business. Of course, all that. But don't get stranded on the mountain top peering heroically to the future. Make sure you pay attention to the bread and butter basics of your organisation – or employ someone who will. I will come back to this critical point in Chapter Eight.

At the height of my messianic fervour about business and purpose in the late 1990s, I opened the pages of the *Liverpool Echo* to bask in the glory of an interview I had given, in which my brilliant insights about enterprise and urban regeneration were laid out for a no doubt grateful readership. Socially innovative business, I asserted, would be the powerful wind which would propel the city out of the doldrums and create work and prosperity for all. There was a photo of me smiling beside the Mersey, every inch the award-winning social enterprise pacesetter. Or so I thought.

Next morning, arriving at work I saw a piece of paper stuck to the door of my office. It was from Stan Riley, one of our machinists and our trade union convenor. 'Liam, I read in the Echo that you will be transforming our city. You can't even get our wages right. Good luck with Liverpool.'

We had been having persistent problems in the finance teams and many of the guys had not been getting the right money in their wage packets. There were also constant issues about tax codes. In a company where many of the workers were paid weekly in cash, this was a big issue. In a social enterprise set up to offer secure work and training for the long-term unemployed, it was a failure of mission and purpose.

I had become intoxicated with my own rhetoric and liked the limelight so much more than chasing down systems failures. I had forgotten to pay close enough attention to the dull but critically important basics of running and leading a business. I much preferred pontificating on stages around the world about the brave new world of purpose-driven enterprise than fixing the plumbing or making sure the plumbers were doing their jobs.

I once saw a banner hanging in Virgin Atlantic's Gatwick Airport training centre which read: *Brilliant basics. Magic touches.* No point in having great cock-tails and films on board if the plane has crashed because a door was left open or there wasn't sufficient fuel in the tanks.

How brilliant are the basics in your business and do you use magic touches to cover up poor fundamentals? Are you much more attracted by flying to Davos to give a keynote on climate change, or fixing the gaps in your supply chains where carbon dioxide pours out?

James Clear, author and renowned phrase maker, put it really well. 'You do not rise to the level of your goals. You fall to the level of your systems. Your goal is your desired outcome. Your system is the collection of daily habits that will get you there.'[23]

Every day's a school day

I'm in my sixties and still figuring out my leadership. I chair a fast-growing global business and I am challenged every day with how most effectively to exercise my authority, how to manage the complex ecosystem of the sometimes competing interests and enthusiasms of fellow directors, investors, staff and senior executives. I've been at this social enterprise game for four decades now and I'm still trying to work out if I

---

[23] www.jamesclear.com/3-2-1/january-2-2020

am making the difference I said I wanted to when I stepped in to this latest hot seat.

Even for grandads, every day is indeed a school day when you want to put purpose at the heart of what you do. My tolerance for the sort of glib self-serving leadership advice which fills the shelves at airport bookshops is zero and I want to break things when I read those 'Do These Ten Things To Be A Great Leader' checklists so beloved by so-called 'influencers' and 'thought leaders' on LinkedIn and Twitter.

Keeping a journal is a habit I have found really helpful in trying to understand myself and my motives, making what sense I can of the rush of time and my place in all of it. I started when I was 20 and couldn't do without it now. I find it a great way of working through problems, giving me space to rant and rave without anyone getting hurt. I write letters to myself and others, make lists of what I am grateful for, or if I'm tired and feeling very uncreative, I simply write out my diary, who I met, what we talked about, what I had for lunch. Lots of quotes from books I have read and the words of leaders I have admired. I recommend journaling to all those I have mentored over the years.

Rereading my journals, I am struck by what an annoying sanctimonious little twerp I often was in my twenties, how so much of what has happened to me I cannot now remember, and how often what seemed so important at work at the time, and about which I worried obsessively, actually wasn't that important after all!

We're at the end of the first part of this book. Thanks for staying with me. In the following chapters I will go deeper into some of the themes we have already touched on and which don't get talked about enough such as loneliness and just how much shit you are prepared to put up with to make the difference you say you want.

Let's jump straight in, shall we? Next up: dealing with bullshit and bullying, of which there is plenty in the world of purpose-led business. Read on.

Gloves-off questions

How are you perceived by your peers? What is the story they would tell about your leadership presence and efficacy? Is it the one you tell yourself?

What are the conversations you've been avoiding with those above and around you who are crucial to the success of your work and the exercise of your leadership?

What do you do?

What could you do?

What's stopping you?

Part Two

Staying alive

'*Some weeks, just staying alive and getting home in one piece on a Friday night is about the biggest win I can achieve – never mind the revolutionary change I was convinced I could spark when I took this job on.*'

Meg, charity CEO

Chapter Five

Bullshit and bullying

Martin Narey worked in the English prison system for 23 years, taking over as Director General at the age of 43 because no one else wanted the job, the deadliest of poisoned chalices in the British civil service. All his predecessors as DG had been very publicly fired by government ministers playing to the worst instincts of the British tabloid press.

Martin is old-school, one of nine children born and bred in a working-class family in industrial Middlesbrough in the north-east of England, imbued with an ethos of hard work and public service by his mother and father.

For seven years, Martin ran a profoundly dysfunctional and violent system, faced every day with shamelessly opportunistic ministers, well-organized and resentful prison staff determined to thwart him and a public indifferent to disgraceful jail conditions.

For the first couple of years Martin felt out of his depth and unequal to the monumental task. 'Every day was bloody miserable,' he told me, 'and everyone said to me "Oh, I couldn't do your job!" What they meant was "You must be some sort of mad bastard to try and change the prison system!" I found the work incredibly rewarding but the job was really hard.'

Martin knew that he couldn't transform the system – maybe no one can – so he set about making important incremental changes to improve the daily life of prisoners and make the system a bit more decent.

Martin's profound commitment to bringing decency into the prison system was seen by the media as pandering to criminals, by the prison officers as undermining their authority and by government ministers as an irrelevance to their priorities of keeping a lid on unrest in the jails and keeping the issue of penal reform out of the public arena. 'I learned early on that if I wanted to make even a little bit of change in a complicated and broken system, I would have to put up with a lot of shit.'

And that he did for seven years – and he didn't get fired. He left the prison service and went on to lead and transform Barnardo's, the UK children's charity. 'Most leaders know what is required to change a culture but have had the courage and staying power knocked out of them. Relentless incremental change is what can get you there. Beware the grandiose innovation plan,' Martin warns.

It's hard

Martin's experiences of the bullshit and bullying of politicians and the media is extreme. The worst of pretty much everything in UK society is to be found in its prison system. I have included his story here because it highlights in the most glaring way the truth that beyond the easy rhetoric of social change and purpose-driven leadership lies much hard slog and dealing with the resistance of others with very different agendas to yours.

I would make it be compulsory for all social wantrepreneurs and influencers to spend half an hour with Martin. It would really benefit all those people who want to find a well-paid job, which they will love doing immediately, with nice people, whilst changing the world, and letting everyone know about it on Instagram.

To 'change the world' is really, really hard work and entails dealing with more setbacks than wins. 'Making a difference' will be more complicated and take much longer than anybody could possibly have imagined during those social enterprise MBA seminars at Said Business School or INSEAD.

I have relished the opportunities to work with leaders like Martin as they try to navigate the challenges of transformation in complex and change-resistant systems. When the lives of homeless people or children in care are at stake, or your work is focused on climate change policy or financial inclusion, leadership is exercised in complex, messy, often highly contested environments where there are no easy answers at all, resources are scarce and resistance is well organized and deeply entrenched.

How do you lead in places like that and not get disillusioned and cynical? How can you avoid putting your mental health and well-being at risk? How do you thrive in that gap between the required brutal realism about the scale of the challenge ahead of you and the idealism and hunger for change that fires your purpose as a leader?

In the rest of the chapter, through the stories of some more of those inspiring people I have the pleasure to accompany as mentor, I offer you some insight into how to not let others knock you off course.

Dealing with Dick

Leading in the public and non-profit sectors is harder than in the private sector. Selling cars or phones is easier than running a public healthcare system or prison estate. The profit motive and demands of share-holders and investors do bring a clarity that is often lacking in the other sectors. 'Are we making money or not?' is a binary question which leadership cannot dodge or fudge, especially in publicly listed companies.

But for the leaders in the corporate world who are driven by a sense of purpose and want to put genuine sustainability into their companies' core strategies, life can be every bit as challenging as it is for the prison governor. Take Kevin, for example.

In early 2018, Kevin called me as I was about to board a plane at Heathrow. He told me that he had had a big promotion and had just walked out of the CEO's office. The CEO had warned him that he was hard to work for, so Kevin should get himself a coach or mentor. He thought of me and picked up the phone.

Kevin had been in the multinational company for several years, and had risen steadily through the ranks, reaching the role of director and leading on an exciting array of important areas across sustainability, innova-tion and corporate citizenship – areas the CEO saw as his legacy issues.

I agreed to work with Kevin as he transitioned into this new bigger role, which he knew would really stretch him. And so it proved. 'Make sure I don't start putting lipstick on pigs,' he said to me. 'Challenge me on delivering real change and value.'

Kevin's CEO – let's call him Dick – is notorious for his utter lack of people skills. In fact, he regards the very idea of 'people skills' as an irrelevant category that gets in the way of decisive leadership.

Dick is, to say the least, a driven man. He would call Kevin at any time of day or night when he wanted something from him, never said please or thank you, regarded emotional intelligence as a contradiction in terms, was alert to the smallest slight, used public bullying and ambush as his management techniques of choice. I came to know Dick well and it felt at times like there were three people in our relationship!

Dick was living proof that for all the talk about authentic or servant leadership, old-school methods are no impediment to getting to the top in British industry. The business had some great HR policies about leadership values and behaviours, innovation and so on and so on. These clearly hadn't been sent to Dick and he'd obviously missed the group hug leadership courses. This is fairly common at the top of most businesses.

Guardian and *New York Times* readers and bouncy congenitally optimistic social entrepreneurs may like to think that the rules of power are changing and that command-and-control behaviour and centralised power plays are out of date. In pretty much all leadership development courses, 'inclusive' or 'authentic' leadership models are the order of the day and hardheaded analysis about how to get and use power to achieve your ends is regarded as passé and somewhat distastefully male.

Perhaps someone should have a word with Trump, Orban, Putin, Xi, Musk, Zuckerberg et al. And let them know the new rules. 'In short, power is not ending,' writes Jeffrey Pfeffer, 'nor are many of its manifestations new. To effectively lead in a world that has not changed as much as many think or expect, people need to understand the basic principles – the rules – of power.' [24]

Kevin and I worked a lot on his meeting tactics and how he would develop his networks inside the company and beyond to build alliances and strengthen his position. It soon became clear that reinforcing his psychological and emotional resilience would be key,

---

[24] Pffefer's book *7 Rules of Power* (Swift Press, 2022) is a must read for some clear-eyed advice about power in the workplace. This quote is from page xix of the Introduction.

as it became very obvious what Dick's MO was. Many is the call I had with Kevin after yet another bruising encounter in the CEO's office.

Bullies win when they get inside your head, and they count on this happening. Keeping Dick out of Kevin's head was a big part of my job as mentor, as was understanding the insidious ways that the poison of Dick's behaviour – much of it in my view a deliberate tactic to wrongfoot people and hide his own insecurities – would seep into Kevin's assessment of himself and his work.

What they say, what they mean

Kevin was experiencing in acute form the gulf between a company's stated values and the actual behaviour of the senior leadership. I am endlessly fascinated by organisational culture and the gap between what leaders say it is – and want you to believe – and what it actually is.

Sometimes this gap explodes into public view. In December 2001, Enron, the energy, commodities and services multinational, went bust, provoking a scandal that would end a few years later with most of its leadership going to jail. In early 2001 I visited Enron's gleaming, phallic Houston headquarters as part of a group of leaders from around the world, keen to learn from this amazing business that was lauded for the entrepreneurial brilliance of its founders. For six years it had topped the Forbes 'Most Innovative Company in America' list.

I genuinely felt lucky to be there and not a little intimidated by the power that seemed to ooze from the wood-panelled walls. Before the high command came into the room to lie through their teeth to us, we were played a very high-production-values video about the business. Over soaring orchestral music, we were taken through the history of the company as images of others who dared to dream and see what could be – including Martin Luther King, Gandhi and Cesar Chavez – flashed before our gullible eyes. In a lovely Hollywood baritone, the narrator slowly enunciated the values of Enron. Respect. Integrity. Communication. Excellence. And:

'We are satisfied with nothing less than the very best in everything we do. We will continue to raise the bar for everyone. The great fun here will be for all of us to discover just how good we can really be.'[25]

As the lights went up I wasn't the only useful idiot in the room wiping away a tear.

---

[25] I swear to God I am not making any of this up.

Anyway, it was all bollocks and 12 months later the world learned what Enron's true values were – Lying, Stealing, Bribery and Corruption.

Ever since that morning in Texas 20 years ago, I have stuck to the belief that any business that uses imagery of Mandela, Mother Teresa or the Dalai Lama is patently lying and hiding something very unpleasant indeed.

How much shit are you prepared to take?

Back to Kevin. He loved the work he was doing and loved being able to put into practice the collegiate, encouraging style of leadership he wanted to be known for. Dick, for all his character flaws and psychodrama, did recognize talent and, in the main, backed Kevin's proposed strategies for the business.

Kevin had taken the decision earlier in his career that he could make a bigger difference in the world at a large business rather than leaving to set up his own company or moving into the non-profit world. 'If I can make 1% change here that impact could be massive in the world,' he told me. One day, after an especially upsetting meeting with Dick, I asked Kevin, 'Just how much shit are you prepared to put up with in order to achieve your 1%?'

Making things change in a big organisation is really tough. It's why there are so few examples of large organisations successfully transforming their cultures, in spite of everything the multimillion-dollar leadership and innovation consultancy industry sells to the corporate market.

Evolving a culture from 'profit first and last' to a business model that embeds environmental sustainability or genuine sex and race equality is the work of many years. The reserves of stamina and resilience required from those – like Kevin – who would step up to build that culture are impossible to overstate.

Most men – and it's usually men in business – who start with a burning zeal to champion change are battered into submission and, by their mid-forties, bend the knee and submit to the prevailing culture of obedience and aversion to risk. Or they leave. I don't for a second judge them for it. I would probably do the same. Head down, pay the mortgage.

Kevin learned the hard way that if you want to be at the top table in a large business you will be there with people who have very different values, behaviours, ambitions and tactics to you – and who don't care much about your precious personal purpose. How quickly you learn to deal with that reality will define how successful you will be.

Some days it did feel for Kevin that the costs were too high for his peace of mind and sleep patterns, and there were times when he felt he could walk away – and there were many times when his wife wanted him to.

Legend has it that when asked what kind of generals he liked, Napoleon replied, 'Lucky ones.' There is no doubt at all that leaders need big strokes of luck in order to succeed, and Kevin's was that Dick decided to retire just as Kevin was beginning to wonder if he could take it any more. God help Dick's wife, was my instant reaction when I heard the news of his decision to leave the business and spend more time at home.

Kevin is tougher and more resilient these days, and in part he has Dick to thank for that. Dick's successor is a very different sort of leader and Kevin is thriving.

But the hard truth is that if you choose to put a purpose beyond profit or career progression, there is a price to pay – especially if your platform is also occupied by others with very different takes on what's important for them and *their* career progression. Genuinely purposeful leadership is not for the fainthearted.

Several of my clients have this image stuck to their office walls or fridges at home, so they don't forget it. This excellent saying, which I believe was coined by a Polish politician in the 90s, I take as a warning to be alert to the temptation to get drawn into the dramas and agendas of others, and so be knocked out of one's own authority, wasting time trying to figure out other people and their reasons.

The people I work with tend to be quite emotionally intelligent and alert to the needs and behaviours of those they lead or to whom they report. They tend also to be people who want to create an inclusive and collegiate style of leadership. They're good people, often working with people who really aren't. (I try to avoid sociopaths and narcissists and, to be honest, they rarely call me.)

The danger is that good leaders end up wasting time and energy responding to the game-playing of others and lose sight of their own path. They can get drawn into the tractor beams of the neediness or malevolence of others and end up being jumped all over by the monkeys of someone else's circus. This was the danger that Kevin faced every time he walked into Dick's office.

The driven, bullying boss or business partner or toxic game-playing leadership-team member cannot be ignored and will have to be dealt with. But I find myself so many times having to remind those I mentor that they cannot control the values or behaviours of others and trying to work out their motivations only gets you so far. What you *can* control is how you react. You can make conscious choices not to be drawn into their circus tent and play their games on their terms. It is very easy to not notice that you are playing someone else's game – so be alert!

I mentored a lovely young guy, let's call him Dave, whose social enterprise business partner – let's call him Pete – just loves to send long bullet-pointed argumentative emails at all hours of the day and night. He's an early riser so Dave would wake up on a Saturday morning to long messages about whatever was that week's drama for Pete.

When I started working with Dave he would continually complain about this inbox warfare, which clearly got under his skin. He would spend too much of his weekends mentally drafting his ripostes and be distracted from his family. I suggested he break this chain and simply tell Pete he wouldn't be answering messages at the weekend or conducting business via long emails. If something needed to be discussed they would do it in their weekly face-to-face meetings.

So long had he been inside Pete's circus tent that Dave had forgotten he could just say no and walk out. This pattern of behaviour was repeated across the range of their interactions. I was convinced it was a conscious strategy by Pete to keep his partner on the back foot, reacting to his agenda and priorities. Dave had the conversation and his weekends are now freer of Pete's mind-monkeys.

'What would Jesus do?'

Kevin's struggle was with his boss, Dick. Simon's was with those for whom he had responsibility. When he took up his first CEO role he inherited a highly toxic divisional head called Nick who oversaw an important part of the charity's revenue generation. This person had been there for years and had seen CEOs come and go. His domain was a no-go area for the rest of the leadership – literally, people didn't go to his part of the building.

In our first few meetings, as this state of affairs became clear to Simon, he wanted to talk about why Nick behaved like this and how he could resolve whatever it was that was going on.

At our second session I asked him why he had not been to the buildings Nick managed. He hummed and hawed until I stopped him. 'You're a bit scared of him, aren't you? You are the CEO and you're allowing your authority to be hedged in by his behaviour. Repeat after me: "Not my circus, not my monkeys". We agreed that, from the very next day, Simon would start to visit 'Nick's' buildings and engage directly with his staff. Nick was angry about that but the spell had been broken and Simon quickly moved his reform strategy on to the agenda.

Simon is a devout Christian and we had many conversations about how his understanding of the teachings of his god about forgiveness and compassion sat with the need for any CEO to have that sliver of ice in the heart that enables unpleasant but necessary work to be done – such as removing toxic and destructive individuals in the interests of the common good of the organisation.

He texted me after the meeting at which he fired Nick, to tell me that he had stopped outside the room beforehand to steel himself for the encounter and thought, 'What would Jesus do?' quickly followed by, 'And what would Liam do?'

My work there was done!

Take heart

Martin Narey's words to me when I asked him to reflect on his time running prisons – 'I found the work incredibly rewarding but the job was really hard.' – really struck me. I think he speaks for many people stuck deep into trying to make a difference in really challenging circumstances. If you feel like that, take heart by knowing you are not alone and what you are experiencing is what it actually *feels* like to be 'making a difference'. If you are experiencing resistance, in your face or more covert, you're probably pushing in just the right place. Keep it up.

Women in leadership pressing for change have a great deal of bullshit to deal with. In the next chapter we will hear from women navigating through organisational cultures designed by men for men.

Gloves-off questions

How much shit are you prepared to take?

'Not my circus, not my monkeys.' Have you been drawn into the dramas and games of others?

Where in your relationships do you need to deliberately reset the boundaries?

Chapter Six

In the theatre of performative male ego

Lucy had a big job in compliance and risk at one of those banks that is forever banging on about how committed to 'inclusion' and 'diversity' it is. The multi-coloured LGBT+ flag flies outside its London HQ.

Lucy was in tears of anger within minutes as she talked to me about the ambient sexism that permeates the male-dominated senior leadership culture. 'They are all individually decent men who would be genuinely appalled to be called out as sexists. But having been the only woman in the room now for a couple of years, I find that I am not as confident and assertive as I was.'

Lucy was losing heart. 'You kind of give up. It's just too much effort to call them out for all those many little ways in which the men rule the roost. I want to leave and just find somewhere where I can be more myself.'

She is surrounded by men who talk endlessly about innovation and change but who change nothing about themselves, or how they work, or how they interact with women, people of colour and younger people.

I posted some of Lucy's words on LinkedIn and the response was instant and dismaying. Some of the stories women told me about their experiences in business were genuinely shocking. Some companies are not so much ambiently sexist as nakedly hostile to women.

Steph, who is in her late thirties, worked at a business widely seen as one of the UK's most successful companies. With a leadership team made up entirely of alpha males it was – and is – a tough place to be a woman.

It is also, Steph acknowledges, a tough and scary place to be a man trying to hold on to a place at the top table. But then again, as she puts it, there's a learning opportunity there, one the alpha males choose to ignore. 'They get to feel something of what women have felt for 1,000 years around male power but it doesn't lead to any empathy or change of behaviour.'

When Steph lamented the lack of female role models at the most senior level to mentor her, she was instructed by her male boss that she had to 'be the change'. Rather than inspiring and empowering her, this was a clear message that no one else felt that change was required, and that if anything did change, it would be her personal career project rather than the company's responsibility.

Faced with this impenetrable status quo, Steph resorted to workarounds. 'The way you end up going is to make the men feel good about themselves. That's the way to get in the door, get the invitation, get on the guest list. I have done that. I'm not proud of it and it doesn't feel good. But as a woman you learn the sexism workarounds. It is a hard truth that as a woman so much of your personal brand is how you look, how you dress. You work with what you've got, don't you? And then feel bad about having to do that.'

The cognitive load Steph ended up carrying inhibited and dampened her impact, and her joy in her work. 'It stops you being quite as great as you could be. You climb inside yourself. The cumulative impact of all these micro-aggressions at work inhibits you.' She left the company.

I'm not the right mentor for everyone, far from it. I recently met with a woman who is a rising star in financial services and was really struggling with the macho culture still all too prevalent in the City. Much as I empathised with her, I said no. I felt that what she really needed was the help of a senior woman who had successfully navigated the waters of a big corporate polluted with sexism. I introduced her to a female friend who's a great coach who had somehow survived in a farcically blokey energy business.

But some of the women who ask me to walk with them for a while are explicit that they want a middle-aged guy specifically to help them understand and deal with the many blokes who surround them in workplaces drenched in sexism and misogyny. In her introductory email, one such woman wrote, 'These guys fill my board room. I need your help to understand how to exercise my authority and not get derailed by insecurities as one of very few women here.'

Pale, male and stale as unique selling point? I'll take it.

When I hear these stories from the women I mentor – and my wife, my daughter, sister, daughters-in-law, women friends and colleagues – about what they are up against on a daily basis, I feel shame and anger. Shame at how I too have been that man whose language and behaviour has upset and obstructed women. My formation as a man was in the 1970s and 1980s and I am still unlearning the misogyny that infected everything in those decades. And anger at seeing how much harder women in leadership still have to work to get ahead, and at the self-serving nonsense of too many of the men in power.

In this chapter I want to amplify as loudly as I can what women in leadership tell me about what it is like to work in a corporate world which has been designed by men for men. All but one of the women I spoke to insisted on strict anonymity for fear of their words damaging their careers. I will use whatever male privilege I have to call out the appalling state of affairs so many women in leadership have to put up with in what one senior woman in a FTSE 100 business brilliantly described as the 'theatre of performative male ego'.

'It's exhausting'

Sexism is not confined to the macho world of big business. Sandra is a CEO in the social enterprise sector and replied to my LinkedIn post echoing the recurrent theme of how hard men make it for women in leadership.

> 'It's exhausting to be that one voice in the room who is having to do all the noticing of this behaviour and calling it out, only to be met with blank faces. I just want to do my job well and not have to be men's guide to the work they need to do – personally – to effect real and useful change.'

I could fill this entire book with messages like these from women in a wide range of sectors and industries.

One more. Mary is the Human Resources Director at a household name FTSE 100 business. She has had a front row seat for many years at the testosterone-fuelled theatre.

My time with her was fascinating, as she unpicked the ways in which senior men navigate their ways through these challenging times. 'Many of the men I work with at the most senior levels do understand that change is required,' she told me, 'but they understand this to be something external to them – getting some women in the leadership meetings, showing enthusiastic support for LGBT events and so on.' The men definitely see the disruption faced by their business and industry as a threat to them, not an opportunity for new ways of leading. 'I doubt that many of the men I work with have asked seriously "what do I need to be doing differently, what does this mean for my behaviour?"'

Sue Garrard – sustainability and PR rock star who sat at Unilever's top table for the better part of a decade – was characteristically blunt with me when we discussed male behaviour in and around the C-Suite. 'Testosterone is the most hazardous chemical in the world, it's bloody lethal stuff. The culture created by men at the most senior levels demands of women so much energy that it is no surprise that they back off. In a team of ten you have to have at least three women there if the men are to become a bit more aware of their behaviour.'

In Mary's company there are only a handful of women in the top leadership group. 'In our leadership meetings the women always sit at the end of the table. The men think "I've allowed you in" rather than, "Am

I ensuring that all voices are genuinely heard?" As a woman, you are in the room but you're not really there.'

I suggested to Mary that the men are not being completely honest with her but she doesn't believe they are acting cynically. 'What I see are men who sincerely believe they have changed when fundamentally their behaviour hasn't.'

The truth is that men at the top have been rewarded for their behaviour; they are successful in the eyes of peers and the world. If it all seems to be working out for you, you must be good at it, right? There are no incentives to unlearn what got them to the top.

Wasted talent

No amount of my mentoring is going to smash the patriarchy. I can help women to work on tactics; to get through that next board meeting and deal with that prat of a non-exec director who just won't shut up and speaks over the few women in the room; to tackle the two blokes who go for a run before the leadership team away days to stich up the agenda; to provide a space to rage and ridicule; and to offer insight into the mind-sets of the motivations and priorities of the middle-aged men who dominate the decision-making.

Both Lucy and Steph decided that leaving was the only way they could deal with what they were experiencing. Mary has accepted the status quo and does what she can to help young women in the company rise. Her pragmatism about where power really lies and what she can do to change that is under-standable. 'I'm not blowing the last few years of my career by confronting head-on the attitudes of men who don't want to hear it.'

Women can be as positive as they like and have as many workplace group meetings as they can fit into their busy days, but unless men become tireless allies to change the culture, it is all so much wasted, frus-trating effort. At this rate we will be having the same argument when my six-year-old granddaughter enters the workforce.

In the words of the former CEO of the Fawcett Society, Sam Smethers, 'Despite much lip service about the importance of having women in top jobs, today's data shows we are still generations away from achieving anything close to equality. We are wasting women's talent and skills.'

Attention: men in leadership

I want to address the men in leadership who might be reading this.

Have you ever come across a leadership team anywhere which, when discussing 'innovation' and 'disruption', asks the question, 'How much of our own power are we prepared to relinquish in order to achieve the "disruptive change" we say all the time is required for our organisation?' Disruption tends to stop just outside the lift to the C-Suite and board room. Funny that.

Most men get to the top not through their brilliance and outstanding performance but because they know how to play the game with the other men and they have demonstrated over time their obedience to the prevailing norms.

Jeffery Pfeffer at Stanford has made a career cutting through the wishful thinking and wilful blindness of leadership gurus and development programmes. According to Pfeffer the data shows that in organisations of all kinds – from multinational corporations to small non-profits – people generally advance through the ranks by pleasing their bosses. The link between job performance and outcomes is surprisingly, and depressingly, weak.

'As long as you keep your boss or bosses happy, performance really does not matter that much,' Pfeffer explains, 'and by contrast, if you upset them, performance won't save you.'

The best way to please bosses? Flattery. And plenty of it. 'Because flattery works and is effective.' A critical component of workplace success and advancement, says Pfeffer, is 'to help those with more power enhance their positive feelings about themselves.' And, let's face it, no one likes their positive feelings about themselves enhanced more than us – middle-aged men.[26]

What I often hear, from men talking about upping the numbers of women on leadership teams and boards – and it is typically delivered with a wise and knowing tilt of the head – is something along these lines: 'Yes we need more women, of course we do, and black people too, but we can't level down, we must only recruit top talent.'

The assumption being made here – which I am always expected to agree with – is that leadership teams and boards are just bursting with fabulously talented middle-aged guys who have made it there solely because of their dazzling skills and unmatched business success and wisdom. Well, sorry lads, but having spent 20 years and more in and out of exco and board meetings, I have rarely been dazzled. Very often I have that feeling Dorothy must have had when she pulled back the curtain to reveal the Wizard of Oz.

There are many great and honourable men atop organisations who *are* good at their jobs and know that part of that is sidestepping macho posturing and being careful not to use their authority in ways that belittle

---

[26] Interview with *The Bulwark*, February 2020.

and limit women. But they are rare. Most men keep their heads down, make the right noises about diversity, may even performatively declare their pronouns, but actually do nothing meaningful to help achieve genuine equality.

Of course not all women are the helpless victims of horrible men. I have mentored people who struggle with oppressive and restricting women bosses. I've encountered women in senior leadership who have kicked away the ladder and blame other women for not showing sufficient grit and application rather than using their authority to take on the systemic and cultural barriers thrown up by the men. But women in such positions are few.

It takes bravery to risk genuine change at personal and organisational levels, especially in the interests of other people. Trouble is that personal courage is drained from men as they ascend the corporate ladder. We exchange courage for cash and status.

David Smith is the former head of HR and culture at Asda, and now a writer and coach. He knows what he's talking about. 'The further up the corporate ladder you go,' he told me, 'the more bravery is drained from you. Even though the trappings of success surround you, perversely it does make you lose confidence. Leadership courage is in short supply and is much more rare than it should be given the challenges facing business.'

Why have all those good intentions about sex equality over the years come to nothing? Why, despite all the talk and PR about 'diversity' and 'inclusion' are the upper echelons so white and male? Because white men are so much better than women and black people? To answer that means confronting the structures and cultures – overt and carefully hidden – which ensure white men promote other obedient white men into positions of power.

'These guys get into their fifties and reach the top of the greasy pole, killing themselves to get there,' observes Sue Garrard, 'and think two things: 1. "Bloody hell is this it? Look at all this shit I have to deal with." And 2. "How am I going to hang on in here?" They get stuck but can't admit it to themselves, or others.'

Sue told me that many of the men she has worked alongside may talk a lot about innovation and change but are actually quietly terrified about the environments in which they now have to lead. 'They are exposed to areas they don't know much about (digital, for example, or sustainability) at a time when they just want to take the cream off the top. Their leadership model has been to be the one who knows all the answers but now more than ever, that simply isn't possible.'

Add to this #metoo and the fallout from Black Lives Matter and you have a lot of men in authority who are stuck and unsure how to behave.

Step up

What I have written here will really rankle with many men. I understand. But if you are a man reading this and thinking, 'Well, I'm not like that, I don't treat women badly, I don't contribute to any ambient sexism or any other kind of bias in my company, I'm one of the good guys' all I can suggest is, have a look around your leadership team and your wider business.

If you see thriving diversity and women at all levels in the organisation with a voice as heard as yours, well done! If not, and your exco and board meetings are dominated by men very much like you, then there is a further question to be faced: *What are you going to do about that?* Not HR, not the board's taskforce on diversity, or the external gender consultants, but *you*. Step up, man.

My editor in her feedback on this chapter encouraged me to end on a positive note, give some encouragement, 'Bit grim isn't it Liam?' I don't want to add to the pile of facile dead words heaped up over the years about 'diversity' and 'equality'. The hard truth is that men in leadership are simply not incentivised in any ways – especially financially – to take the risk of breaking from the pack and calling for more radical options to address the ridiculous state of affairs we have created.

But if we're serious about building businesses to make a change in the world, that change, like charity, must begin at home, in our own board rooms and senior teams.

Training sessions, inspirational speakers, coaches, books, residential group hugs, rainbow wristbands and flag waving have all failed to make much of a dent in the male dominance of business leadership. If I was chairman of any of the businesses I've written about in this chapter, I would send out this memo:

> 'Guys. You have 18 months to make your teams less blokey and white and hostile to women. I am open to whatever tactics you want to use within reason to achieve this. 50% of your bonus will be linked to this goal and if you fail to achieve it your chances of promotion will be zero.
>
> I appreciate that some of us might do the right thing for the wrong reasons. But at least we'll be trying to do the right thing. Because right now clearly not enough of us are.'

Gloves-off questions

What role are you playing in the theatre of performative male ego?

If you got my memo, what practically would you do over the next 18 months to step up?

Chapter Seven

On loneliness and mental health

This text pinged on to my phone one day from Robin, a first-time CEO in a troubled business: 'I have had 8 meets today. 68 people. I have never in my life felt so on my own.'

Robin had been referred to me several weeks previously when he was in considerable distress. Through no fault of his, a business partner had abruptly left the company – a very socially minded design agency – and there was no one else to take the reins of the business but Robin, an introverted, nerdy product designer. Suddenly overseeing the business was his responsibility, a business with very tight cashflow, some big liabilities and a restless and worried staff team of 30 people.

141

Number one priority was to work out what he really wanted. 'What do you want?' I asked him. 'Not what you feel you should do or what obligations you feel you are under, but what do you, Robin, want in your life now?'

Things at work had gone in a totally unexpected direction but he retained the ability, I reminded him, to decide what to do with his life. He had choices, some admittedly quite tough ones. He listened to my advice and took a couple of days off to talk to his wife about the call he had to make, which deeply affected both of them. He chose to stay and, despite his fears about his abilities and what his mind told him about his useless-ness with money, he stepped fully into the CEO role. In our mentoring we turned to the opportunities he had to build out a board and reshape the company.

The morning after I received his text, we spoke on the phone. 'Liam, you've been dead helpful but you should have warned me about the loneliness, mate. That's the hardest bit of this for me.'

Robin was right. I should have warned him about the loneliness. So that's why I'm including this section. To warn you about the loneliness, a subject about which there is nowhere near enough discussion and honesty in leadership books.

Loneliness

If job descriptions were honest they would run something like:

Chief Executive Officer

This company offers a competitive salary and generous pension scheme.
We have ambitious plans for growth.
We have a commitment to diversity and inclusion.
We might even get a woman of colour on our Board one day.
You'll often feel intensely lonely and exposed in this job and overwhelmed by the scale of the challenges, especially if this is your first time.
Keep it to yourself though.

Many are those new CEOs who have badly underestimated the distance between being Number 2 and being Number 1. You are being paid to be the one who goes to bed on a Friday night worrying about the business, whose radar can never be turned completely off.

If you are promoted from within, relationships change with everyone in the organisation, and people behave differently around you. You are now the boss and their jobs and prospects depend on keeping on the right side of you. You have the power and they don't. That makes for an asymmetric relationship, no matter how chummy and approachable you want to be or think you are. This was exactly Robin's experience.

As you survey your exco team you may have to be planning the forced exit of some of them in order to achieve your goals. This means there will always be a big part of you that you must keep at a distance.

You are hardly likely to want to share your anxieties and vulnerabilities with your chair and board. 'Yes, there is something I want to raise under AOB: I feel bloody scared and sometimes have no idea what I should be doing.' Not going to happen, is it? Such honesty would be career-ending.

There will be times when you feel terrible, battered from pillar to post, confused by the relentless complexity of what you face, totally unable to pick up the signal in the noise – and with people above and below you looking to you for clarity and confidence, who are perhaps feeling even more anxious than you. With money – other people's money – at stake and jobs on the line, you must do your leading in an era of social media and Glassdoor, and the fear of failure and the loneliness intensifies. You must be able to put on a positive face in the face of adversity. If you can't then you're not going to succeed because you have to be able to convince people to stay with you. This too can add to the sense of loneliness.

There are so many relationships to manage and competing needs to square. It's what makes leadership thrilling and, when you get it right, deeply fulfilling. But if the buck stops with you, in a very real sense indeed, you're on your own. During the Covid pandemic I know that many leaders felt the isolation intensely on top of the weariness and frustration of dealing with the mash-up of work and home.

The key is knowing that these bouts of intense isolation and loneliness don't make you a bad leader, they simply show you are all too human. If you expect it, it helps you deal with it. Building a support structure around you when you get to that lonely place is vital. Keeping physically fit, managing the diary, staying plugged into what gives you energy, having a clear strategy about which you have sufficient confidence.

This is where mentoring can be really helpful. Find someone with whom you can be totally free to be yourself and express what you think is unsayable in the workplace or maybe even to your closest loved ones.

I wonder if loneliness is even more acute for entrepreneurs who have created their own businesses. Reid Hoffman, the founder of LinkedIn, certainly thinks so. He has spoken and written honestly about the anxiety and loneliness he has experienced.[27] 'You will feel lonely, day after day,' he says, 'seriously, seriously lonely. Your people don't want you to explain your balanced investment thesis, lay out your strategy, and explain how you're managing the risk factors. They just want you to say, "We're going to win."'

The cult of the superhero entrepreneur who can do it all remains strong, especially amongst young men who fear that talking about how they really feel will be seen as weakness. Hoffman again: 'I worried many times that if I confessed my fear, uncertainty, and doubt, that I'd be undercutting my chances of success. After all, doesn't everyone extol the virtues of grit, persistence, and never giving up?'

The answer, advises Hoffman, is not to go it alone. 'Rely on your allies, rely on your friends, rely on your colleagues, rely on your mentors, and rely on the people who are close to you. Entrepreneurship is a team sport.'

Turns out that Robin is a pretty good CEO and now, with an excellent chairman who has brought in new investment and networks, the company is doing well both in terms of profitability and quality of impact. Robin demonstrates that there are many ways to be a leader, and his is the quiet unassuming style.

---

[27] *Greymatter* blog 15th December 2020.

The important part is that he has done the work and *chosen* how to lead.

Mental health is a leadership issue

As part of my preparation for writing this chapter, I looked back in my journal to my mid-thirties when I first became a CEO in a social enterprise in Liverpool. I was genuinely shocked by the deep anxiety about the pressures and loneliness of leadership that I found in those pages. I think I was properly depressed and I used Jameson's to self-medicate.

Thirty years ago, no one – and I mean *no one* – talked about their mental health, especially award-winning social enterprise leaders like me – male, needy, insecure, making it up as I went along, who would never dream of uttering one word about my vulnerability and anxiety.

Today, thank goodness, there is a lot more openness about mental health across society. Members of the British Royal family talk on the TV about their mental health and raise money and awareness for charities. There are hundreds of apps available to download and investors are busy looking for more mental health tech businesses in which to invest. The Covid pandemic accelerated the acceptance of online digital mental health support by 10 years, as isolation and anxiety became hot topics that could not be ignored.

But public mental health services remain woefully underfunded and the stigma around mental ill health is far from defeated.

At Togetherall we run an anonymised global online platform available every day of the year, offering peer-to-peer support and moderated by our brilliant squad of mental health professionals. We welcome many thousands of students, soldiers, corporate executives, health service patients, sports people, oil rig workers, all who are seeking support and willing to offer it to others.

On the Togetherall platform, more than 60% of our members tell us they have never shared their mental health struggles with anyone in their families or at work. Six out of ten.

There are some courageous individuals who have made it their mission to get the conversation going in business leadership about anxiety and depression. Geoff McDonald in the UK is a pioneer and doing great work on this.[28] Following his breakdown when he was a senior executive at Unilever he has made it his life's mission to break the taboo around mental health struggles.

---

[28] geoffmcdonald.co.uk

'I want people in organisations to feel they have the choice to put their hands up if they are suffering from anxiety or depression, just as they would if they were suffering from a physical illness.' Don't we all, Geoff. But the hard truth is that there are still many miles to go.

Above a certain level of seniority, to speak about your anxiety or depression honestly means big trouble for your career development. A C-Suite exec at a well-known global media business told me that in spite of a raft of excellent healthcare options available for staff, if *he* were to speak about his personal struggles with anxiety and drink, he'd be toast. He would only speak to me for this book if I guaranteed anonymity. 'Everyone around that executive committee table has signed off our pretty great mental health and well-being policies for staff. And everyone around that executive committee table knows that to express our own anxiety and mental problems would be to commit career suicide.'

One social entrepreneur who was active in Africa and who I turned down for mentoring, told me that it was a self-indulgent first-world luxury to worry too much about one's own mental health when so many people have far worse struggles with homelessness and hunger. 'How useful will you be to them,' I asked, 'if you're burned out and empty inside? Haven't people suffered enough without putting up with you at the end of your tether? Get over yourself.'

Looking out for our own mental health and the mental health of those we work with is a must. This is even more the case with those who want to change the world. That sense of mission and purpose can all too easily become a burden, and admirable drive and persistence sour into anxiety and depression.

In 2016 Michelle Morgan, co-founder and CEO of Livity, one of London's coolest, multi-award-winning and best-known purpose-driven marketing agencies, closed a gruelling but successful multi-million-pound investment raise and agreed an ambitious plan for growth and enhanced impact in the lives of young people.

On the outside everything was hunky dory. But Meesh was really struggling.

'I was experiencing many challenges that year, professionally, physically, and personally,' she told me, 'but it was the years of fighting and proving that you could place equal importance on purpose and profit that were taking their toll.' Meesh felt burdened by the responsibility, not just for her team and the young people coming through Livity, but for all young people everywhere.

Michelle ignored the headaches, the insomnia, the excessive drinking and kept on keeping on, day after day, the joy and excitement drained empty from her work. She had never felt so alone. And then one day she couldn't do it any longer, she was burnt out. She felt constant panic and couldn't even bring herself to walk into her Brixton HQ where she had such fun and excitement for so many years. Her passion and purpose had completely burnt out too. 'This was a devastating moment for me,' she writes in *Own Your Awkward,* 'and that's when the anxiety started escalating rapidly and I entered what felt like a constant state of terror and insomnia.'

Under a cloud of shame and embarrassment, Michelle wasn't talking about how she was feeling ('After all, leaders should be strong and resilient all the time shouldn't they?'). Her mental state spiralled downwards, and when she did find the courage to talk about the difficulties she was experiencing, she finally received a diagnosis of clinical depression and severe anxiety.

'We all have mental health,' she counsels. 'It's not fixed and we're all vulnerable to developing poor mental health. When we don't talk about it, that's when it escalates.'

Today, Meesh has a new mission: to help businesses have better and braver conversations about mental health in the workplace. She is also developing new business ideas (she is after all an entrepreneur). Her message for us: 'Mental Health is a leadership issue, those who place the importance of mental health at the centre of their culture and business plans will win the race to attract and retain brilliant people.' Please read her book.[29]

At Oxford University, Dr Henry Majed, founder of mymind.co.uk has been carrying out some fascinating research into the mental health of 'purpose driven/ sustainability practitioners' as the challenges of the climate crisis and other pressing societal issues move up the agenda in their businesses.

'The desire to create a positive impact can be overwhelming in the current global climate,' he told me. 'An endless cycle of negative environmental news, reports of inequity and conflict, can result in feeling helpless. A sense of always more to do, and our own unforgiving expectations, becomes overwhelming.'

Put on your own oxygen mask first

Changing the world is long-haul work and you will probably not see the full impact of what you do in your lifetime. Sustainability veteran John Elkington has

---

[29] Michelle Morgan, *Own Your Awkward: How to Have Better and Braver Conversations About Our Mental Health* (Welbeck Balance, 2021).

been at it for 50 years: 'Major paradigm shifts take 70 to 80 years to complete. And we're well over 60 years into this one, so the next 15 years will see change go off the scale, though not automatically in the right direction. Which is why I will still be needed!'

The hard truth is that you will for sure experience more setbacks and disappointments than game-changing breakthroughs. Your successes will be partial and contingent. This is a long game. Looking after yourself, therefore – especially your mental health and well-being – is a key practice for any purpose-driven changemaker. You want to help others, you must look after yourself. It is not a luxury activity or privilege to take your mental health seriously. To not do so is reckless for you and those you lead. There is a good reason why on a plane you fix your own oxygen mask before helping others.

Impatient changemakers can do great things in the world. They can also be their own worst enemies and nightmares for those who work with them, invest in their ideas – and those who marry them. In our final chapter you'll meet Matt whose commitment to changing the world was hurting him and those he loved. He's a maniac, he needed a minder.

Gloves-off questions

Are you lonely in your leadership? Be honest.

How would you rate your mental health? Do you experience persistent trouble sleeping, feelings of panic, of not being in control, of oppressive anxiety for the mission of your organisation?

Michelle Morgan talks about the BRAVE talking framework. Use it, please.

Be aware – of how you are feeling and coping with life.
Remember – you are not alone.
Ask for help – from someone you trust.
Value yourself – you are not a burden.
Explore what helps – we are all different.

Chapter Eight

Maniac and minder

'So, Matt, when did you last make love with your wife?'

Long pause.

'Dunno. Last August. Something like that.'

'Nearly a year ago?'

'Shit, yeah. A year ago. That's not good is it?'

I don't make a habit of straying into the bedrooms of those I mentor but with Matt I had to go there. He had been telling me about his chaotic, over-scheduled life, running a sustainability tech firm, trying and failing to manage a staff of 20 and raise his next round of funding. He was loved by his clients, who found his 'all over the place' radical behaviours charming, alongside his undoubted talent and passionate drive. So far he had always delivered for his clients but the price he and those closest to him were paying, especially his wife, was getting too much. Things were so bad that he got over his pride to get in touch with me and ask for help.

The mind map I got him to draw about the shape of his life and commitments was the messiest I've seen and included a house with a little girl in it – his daughter – with a sad face.

'Why's she sad?' I asked.

'Because she doesn't see enough of her dad.'

'How would you describe you work/life balance,' I asked sarcastically.

'I don't have a life.' He had tears in his eyes now.

Matt was an extreme case of what I call the 'severely gifted', his desire to change the world, and sense of time running out to do it, his guilt about his 'privilege', and his wild talent, combined to corrode his life with a toxic drivenness which had alienated him from the woman he loved most in the world.

My first piece of advice to Matt was that he book a hotel and go away for a long weekend, leaving his phone in Dalston, and just let the world get on with itself whilst he, ahem, reconnected with his wife. A month later I got a photo of two sets of feet entwined at the end of a bubble bath.

In *Bleak House* Charles Dickens created the very memorable character of Mrs Jellyby who is so obsessed with her charity work in Africa that she can't see that her own family is falling apart around her. Dickens coined the brilliant phrase 'telescopic philanthropy' and it is something that today's purpose-driven leaders need to be very wary of. Matt had an acute case of Mrs Jellyby Syndrome and our mentoring work became mainly about how he could continue to devote his working life to addressing the climate emergency without losing those he loved.

Stephen Lloyd – my mate and lawyer until his untimely death in 2014 – once told me, 'Every business needs a maniac and a minder.' Without the maniac nothing innovative or surprising would get created in the face of naysayers and vested interests. Without the minder, brilliant ideas will not survive for long if the dull but important work of systems and process-building doesn't happen.

Matt was the maniac but he needed a minder – someone to take on the dull but important stuff – to enable him to focus on what he loves and is so good at and what brings him alive.

'This work of change is addictive'

If you think you can end homelessness, or stop climate change, or you have the solution to a problem which has eluded everyone else, you have to have something of the maniac in you – driven, not willing to hear 'no', pushing on when others have had enough, obsessive, unreasonable, sometimes a real pain in the neck for those around you.

But – sounding like a very old man now – I have seen scores of these sorts of social entrepreneurs and leaders over the decades who burn bright for a few years and then – poof! – gone, leaving not much behind them, except lots of resentment, disappointed investors and unpaid bills.

Don't be that leader.

Karen Lynch who spent 10 years turning around the fortunes of Belu Water is now a sought-after mentor and speaker about leadership and social change: 'This work of change is addictive and I have to watch that in myself. I am driven by a fear of failure and am attracted to solving other people's problems. You can become obsessed and that hurts you and those around you.'

If you want to change the world, you want to make a lasting difference through your work, then you do really need to look after yourself. Not only are driven, *'look at me I'm saving the world, I'm so exhausted'* leaders very boring they tend not to last the course and drive support away.

You can't however outsource it all. You have to manage the struggle between the maniac and the minder within you. Your inner minder who notices when you're out of flow, anxious, running on empty. Who knows that taking a holiday and switching off the phone is every bit as important as that next meeting with a funder or potential partner. Who knows indeed that your chances of landing that new investor or attracting that world-class CFO you need so badly are increased if you are taking care of yourself because the best of you turns up to the meeting, not the driven, sleep-deprived maniac!

Build teams which mix the maniac and minder mindsets. Good minders can help maniacs to flourish long term rather than crashing and burning. But be careful. As Martin Narey who ran the prison service told me, 'I worked with an ex-army Chief Officer in a tough prison who was brave enough to promote an unusually bright but occasionally manic prison officer Alan to a key post. He got the prison-workshop to make a little wooden sign for Alan's desk on which were the letters WWFFSW. He told Alan to read that sign every day that he, the Chief, wasn't at work. It stood for *Whoa, Whoa, For Fuck's Sake Whoa*.'

No easy answers

Let me be clear. I have no magic solution for you. If you commit yourself to something that is really important, that matters deeply to you, to something much bigger than earning a salary or pulling down dividends, then that comes with a price in terms of cognitive and emotional load and will put extra strain on your well-being and the relationships which matter to you. There's no getting away from that.

It's harder to switch off if your job involves supporting refugees or finding the money to keep a women's refuge open. If you are deeply involved in developing technology which may have a large-scale impact on how we deal with the effects of climate heating then you don't just clock off at 6pm and go to the pub. There will always be what looks like a good reason to cancel that two weeks in France camping with the kids.

Donna – who rose to senior authority in child safeguarding work – put it very bluntly to me after her bitter divorce. 'I was too busy saving kids, I couldn't save my marriage.'

I too often got the balance wrong in my own life and I regret not being more available for my young children in my thirties when I was trying to figure out how to lead a purpose-driven business. As a recovering Catholic, I am pretty good at guilt.

When I was a CEO with Jamie Oliver I travelled a lot and was often away from home and pretty much every day, late home. Walking in the house one night my daughter walked towards me ignoring my 'good evening', brushed past and went upstairs in silence. I suddenly realised that I had completely forgotten about the parents' meeting at her school earlier that evening which I had promised to attend. As I trotted out my pathetic excuses (again) to my wife Maggie – 'something *really* important came up at work' type of thing – she interrupted me.

'Do you know the problem with you, Liam? You're never here and when you are here you're never really fucking here!'

Karen Lynch again: 'As a social entrepreneur you obsess about your social mission. But the rest of the world around you isn't obsessed with you, they're worrying about what to put in their kids' sandwiches for lunch and can they pay their electricity bills this month.' You are obsessing about the world and its problems but the world is not obsessing about you and your purpose.

Karen advises to watch out for the 'superhero syndrome' because that will really do your head in. 'It's hard. Being able to find some kind of serenity whilst pushing to the limits what's in your control but accepting many things are not within your control. When you have a team – and you have to have a great team – that brings challenge too because you must accept a loss of perfection, people won't always do it the way you would, but you have to get out of the detail and that means giving up some control. That's hard for those who want to change the world because we think we know best!'

The good news

Opting to make a difference in your work by tackling messy, complex, fast-changing social problems can be thrilling and deeply satisfying. But it should only be done with your eyes wide open and fully accepting the downsides.

But here's the good news, the more you build your resilience, the more you work on understanding what really drives you, the more you understand what gives you energy and life, the more effective you'll be and the more people will listen and follow you.

Resilience is not just about good mental attitude and taking your significant other off to a posh hotel once a year. It is about getting the basics right. Managing your time and energy well, building robust businesses with high-performing teams, with well-constructed boards offering you the right blend of support, encouragement, accountability and challenge. A great board will be of much more use to you when you really need them – and trust me you will

– than your ability to get through 15 hour days on little sleep.

With Matt, we started with the basics. We looked at how his diary got filled with appointments and meetings. Turns out his PA was mirroring his chaotic approach and stuffing his week with activity leaving no time for reflection, falling in knackered late on a Friday night, neither use nor ornament for his family. Use of time and who has control over the diary is something you must constantly monitor. If you are lucky enough to have PA or secretary, brief them regularly about what is important and who gets straight into the diary and who will have to wait.

I asked Matt, 'If there was one thing you could drop right now and never have to do again what would it be?'

Without a second's hesitation: 'Managing people. I hate it.'

Over the coming months Matt, with my encouragement and challenge, reordered the ways the company works, and relieving him of the chore – as he saw it – of running senior management meetings, doing appraisals (we all hate these, don't we?). Matt is a provocateur and fire starter who had allowed himself to drift into pretending to be a managing director, going through the motions of running a company which just drained energy and focus from him. Luckily there was a seriously talented young woman in his team who stepped up brilliantly into the vital management role freeing Matt up to do what he is great at – and the world needs.

Off the cross, please

Here's the thing: you can't save the world. Sorry. I can confidently urge you down from that cross. But you *can* do great work, make a positive lasting difference in the field of your choice, create a brilliant company, if you give equal weighting to looking after yourself as you do to the social issue you are tackling. Sounds easy, but it isn't. Your impatient anxious concern for some future better state – for the world, your start-up, your charity, your corporate – can too easily rob you of your ability to live in the present moment and be *really* there for yourself and others.

The inability of so many of those I mentor to be able to relish the present, dwell appropriately on achievements – in all their imperfections and incompleteness – is striking.

Recently one of my clients, Terry, a C-Suite leader in a car manufacturer, couldn't wait to get through the opening pleasantries to get to the problem about which he wanted my point of view.

'Hold on there' I told him, 'what's been going on since we last met, anything interesting?' He made that face one makes when trying to dredge up something from the deepest recesses of our minds and then told me,

'Oh yeah. We signed off our electric car strategy for the next decade.'

'Wow,' says I, 'that's amazing. Hang on. You sat in the meeting where a genuinely historic decision was made that could have huge consequences for reducing emissions across the world?'

'Yeah.'

'And we've been talking for three years about how you align purpose and platform and how you make a difference and you forgot to tell me that you were there at what might be the high point so far of your purpose-driven career?'

'I ran the meeting, Liam.'

Reader, I nearly slapped him.

We then spent half an hour reflecting on the road that he had travelled to this point, the obstacles encountered and overcome, the dark moments when it seemed like he was making no progress, the late-night calls between us when he was considering quitting.

I've got form on this. I am terrible about inhabiting the now and enjoying the wins before rushing on to the next thing. It's easy see it in others, quite something else to see it and sort it out in oneself. Here is the mentor's dirty little secret: sometimes we encourage others to do that which we fail to do enough of ourselves. Don't tell anyone, will you? It is actually one of the reasons why I like mentoring so much: it is as much a reminder to me about what's important as it is to those I have the privilege of accompanying.

Run, rest and romance

Patrick is a deeply impressive and talented young man I mentor who came to me in 2021 with a very severe case of Social Entrepreneur Mania. We had the maniac/minder conversation and he wrote a list (he loves lists) which I share with his permission:

> Do: stay angry at the injustices of the world
> Don't: let that anger poison me and those I love and work with
> Do: give myself permission to work really hard
> Don't: expect others to match me
> Do: let my team do what they are great at
> Don't: sweat the small stuff and interfere
> Do: put time in diary to run, rest and romance
> Don't: forget to say thank you and enjoy my successes

I like the simplicity and directness of Pat's list and it is a good stab at distilling the maniac/minder conundrum into clear actions to try and get to a healthy balance and not burn out himself or his people.

Gloves–off questions

Are you more maniac or minder?

Where is your commitment to making a difference damaging you and your relationships? What will you do about that?

How will you get better at celebrating your wins and not allowing your desire for a better future to get in the way of living your life NOW to the full?

Reread Pat's 'Run, rest, romance' list. What will your Do's and Don'ts be now?

And, finally...

'*Now is the time to get serious about living your ideals. How long can you afford to put off who you really want to be? Your nobler self cannot wait any longer.*'

Epictetus

A s I sit down to write the conclusion to this book the world seems a very grim place indeed.

Wars and rumours of wars. Much of Europe – including parts of London – on fire because of the extreme heat of the climate crisis. Water and gas in short supply and prices rising across the board threatening the precarious livelihoods of so many.

Last night I received this WhatsApp from a wonderful young woman Cath who I have the delight of mentoring, in response to a rather downbeat message from me about the state of the world.

'Our efforts seem so trivial, pathetic, in face of what's happening but we can't give up Liam. I can't stop Putin but I won't let him stop me. I can't change the world probably but I can change the bit I'm in. We double down old man, we double down.'

Pessimism, as poet Salena Godden wrote, is for lightweights.

I hope the changemakers' stories I have shared in this book have encouraged you to double down – but to do so with your eyes open, whether you are running your own social business (or want to) or trying to make a difference in a corporate or public sector organisation.

Understand why you do what you do and keep it under regular review. Don't let your mind get you and let anxiety or a feeling that you're not enough or don't deserve to be in the room. Everyone – apart from the psychos – feels like an imposter sometimes. Look after your health – mind and body – and stay plugged in to what gives you energy – because now more than ever you will need that to remain resilient and at your best.

Take care with the leadership authority you have been given and claimed and don't allow the games and dramas of others to derail you. Say after me, *'not my circus, not my monkeys'*.

Pay attention to you how you feel. Remember recurrent irritability, anxiety, boredom can be signals that it is time to move on, that the platform upon which you are pursuing your purpose is no longer the right one for you. If it feels like it isn't then take some time to dig into what you want next and where now might be the place for you to make that difference in the world. What do you do? What could you do? What's stopping you?

Work on your courage. Remember Chen's question, '*How will I know if I'm falling or flying?*' Sometimes you won't and that can be what bravery feels like. And sometimes you are just falling and you'll have to pick yourself up and start again. Shit happens, dear reader, shit happens.

Get yourself an honest and straight-talking mentor to help you with your clarity and courage as you make your difference in the world. Someone willing, when necessary, to take the gloves off. You will need different sorts of mentors at different stages in your career. You might be lucky enough to find one who can walk with you over many years. I have a couple of these relationships and I value them very highly. But sometimes a mentor is just for Christmas, giving you a short-term intervention to help get you unstuck or help with a very specific challenge.

Mentoring is no magic bullet for anything but finding the right mentor can help you navigate better the complexities, contradictions and conflicts which every leader has to deal with. In these troubling and bewildering times perhaps the need for mentoring counsel and support has never been greater.

Tom is a Chief of Staff at a global brand, a huge and demanding leadership role. I have accompanied him for more than two years through many dizzying ups and downs and the surreal existential threat of Covid-19 to the very existence of the business. I asked him to sum up the value of mentoring.

> 'Working weeks can often feel like diving headfirst in at the deep end on Monday morning (or Sunday evening?), swimming as fast as you can for five days before eventually coming up for air and clawing your way out on a Friday evening. For me, mentoring is about improving your swimming stroke, remembering to breathe on the way and also trying to enjoy the experience.'

A good mentor will get that balance right between offering you support and encouragement and challenging you and holding your feet to the fire. Too much support and nothing changes, too much challenge you'll back off. The goal is to help you grow – in confidence, in self-knowledge, in the quality and scale of impact, in understanding of what truly motivates you.

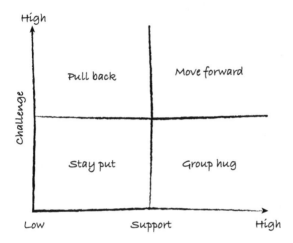

I have had many superb mentors and coaches over the years who have helped shape who I am and how I try to make a difference in the world.

One of those mentors was Muhammad Yunus. It really wasn't the huge things that he has done in his amazing career but he was for me a role model in how to align personal integrity with a deep and relentless passion for justice and equity. Let me end our time together in this book with a couple of stories about Yunus which I believe highlight the behaviour of someone who is making a true and lasting difference in the world.

I first came across Yunus through his book *Banker to The Poor*. At the time – in the mid-90s

– I was struggling to find my feet as the CEO of a purpose-led business. Pre-internet and social media and long before the well-oiled global social entrepreneur ecosystem we have today, reading about what Yunus was achieving gave me the belief that it was possible to dramatically scale impact-first enterprises, and serve millions of people.

I didn't meet Yunus until many years later in my late forties, when I ran a social innovation event in Bangladesh in partnership with Grameen. This led to me taking on the chair role of the Friends of Grameen, a worldwide solidarity network established to counter the vicious anti-Yunus propaganda spewing out of the deeply corrupt Hasina regime in Dhaka. This work carried us to 10 Downing Street and the US Capitol.

Nearly 70 at that time, Yunus was a ball of relentless fizzing energy. I hosted his visits to London and was deeply impressed with his drive, passion and humility. I saw at close quarters how he gave as much of himself to ordinary people as he did to heads of state and celebrities.

One day, striding through early morning London to get to an important meeting at the Foreign and Commonwealth Office, I noticed he was no longer beside me. I turned around to see he had stopped to chat to a Bangladeshi guy who was handing out the free *Metro* newspaper. 'We'll be late if we don't get a move on,' I said.

Yunus ignored my entreaty. 'This man's mother was one of our borrowers. Take a picture.'

Yunus made sure the newspaper guy was happy with the photo and I was asked to ensure I would email it to him as soon as I could. We were late for the FCO gig.

The incident reminded me of the truism that you can get a good sense of people's character by the way they treat waiters.

At the end of a long day, as Yunus signed books and posed for selfies with a line of 128 young people (yes, I counted them), I was busily planning the following day's schedule. We can get out of here by 11.30pm, I thought to myself, be in bed by midnight and up for the BBC Radio 4 interview at 6am. Our car was warming up outside and I was relishing the prospect of the little bottle of red wine I would grab from the minibar when we got back to the hotel in Marylebone.

As – finally! – we walked out of the Aga Khan Centre, Yunus said we should walk back and get some air. Inwardly groaning, I told the driver to leave. Just then, Yunus spotted a curry restaurant. 'Let's eat, Liam.'

'It'll be shut,' I said. *Please God let it be shut.*

We crossed the street to look in the window. The manager was clearing up and waved me away. He then did a double take as he recognised Yunus (who is a very well-known public figure in Bangladesh). He opened the door, grabbed Yunus's arm and in we went.

Having sat us down, the manager ran to the back of the restaurant. Seconds later, Bengalis in chefs' whites and clogs teemed out of the kitchen, incredulous that Professor Yunus – Professor Yunus! – himself was there. For the next couple of hours, as dish after dish emerged from the kitchen, I was called upon to take umpteen photos that were immediately texted back to families in Chittagong.

It was a joyous occasion and our gracious host, Faisal, kept me topped up with red wine. Needless to say, Yunus was already waiting in the hotel lobby the next morning, as fresh and serene as you like, when I tumbled out of the lift looking (and feeling) as if I'd been dragged through a hedge backwards.

It was Yunus who consolidated my belief in the power of stories. He has a tremendous facility with words and is a compelling storyteller and phrasemaker. He has a brilliant ability to cut through the noise by using simple language about the injustice of global poverty and the structures which oppress people. His storytelling is a key reason why he engages so many people all over the world.

Yunus talks about a future in which people will visit Poverty Museums – as today we visit Holocaust

Museums – and be appalled and baffled that for so long we allowed fellow human beings to die of preventable disease and malnutrition, in a world of plenty.

Picking up the Nobel Peace Prize in 2006, Yunus gave a great speech. 'We get what we want,' he said to the assembled great and good, 'or what we didn't refuse... We wanted to go the moon. We went there. We achieve what we want to achieve. Let us join hands to give every human being a fair chance to unleash their energy and creativity.'

If you had the chance tomorrow morning to address such an audience, what would be your stories of leadership purpose and ambition?

Recommended reading and watching

There is so much rubbish published about leadership and change management. Every year the books pour out. Hopefully, I haven't written one like that! But there are some belters out there. Of course I recommend all the books I referenced in the preceding chapters.

I asked the contributors to this book and a selection of my mentoring clients for their recommendations for you, books which had made a lasting impression on them. Here's what they came back with in no particular order.

James Timpson recommends *Happiness: Your Route Map to Inner Joy* by Andy Cope (John Murray, Learning, 2018)

Martin Narey's recommendation is *Michael O'Leary: A Life in Full Flight* by Alan Ruddock (Penguin, 2008)

Says Martin: 'Well, of course, I'd precede any list by warning of the amount of bilge in leadership writing and the need not to become intimidated by stories of "transformation". This is the exception for me, because it's a story of hard grind and trying to make things a tiny bit better each day.'

The One Thing by Gary Keller (John Murray Learning, 2014)

Keller argues the key to extraordinary success is focusing daily on the 'One Thing' that's most important for achieving your goal, rather than scattering yourself in many directions.

The Hard Thing About Hard Things by Ben Horowitz (Harper Business, 2014)

There is no recipe for those hard situations in business. This book is a collection of advice and first-hand experiences to help company operators deal with the hard times.

Only The Paranoid Survive by Andrew Grove (Broadway Business, 1996)

How to deal with crises and turn them to your advantage.

Invisible Women: Exposing Data Bias in a World Designed for Men by Caroline Criado Perez (Chatto & Windus, 2019)

It's in the title!

Jane Clubb – who coached me at critical times in my career and convinced me that I'm not a coach but a mentor – recommends:

Executive Coaching with Backbone and Heart by Mary Beth O'Neil (John Wiley & Sons Inc, 2007)

Touchpoint Leadership – Creating collaborative energy across teams and organizations by Hilary Lines and Jacqui Scholes-Rhodes (Kogan Page Ltd, 2013)

Bad Leadership: What it is, How it happens, Why it Matters by Barbara Kellerman (Harvard Business School Press, 2004)

Because leadership makes a difference those of us who desire to make the world a better place must do what Tutu did. We must come to grips with leadership as two contradictory things: good and bad.

Several people recommended watching Brené Brown's 2012 TEDxHouston talk *The Power of Vulnerability*. I strongly urge you to watch Maff Potts on the meaning of life in his 2019 talk *The Power of Friends and Purpose* (it's on YouTube). 'What if it doesn't work? What if we fuck up?'

All About Love by bell hooks (William Morrow, 2000) was also highly recommended.

And one person said Bruce Springsteen's autobiography is a must read.

Thanks

First of all, thank you to all those I have had the privilege of mentoring who have allowed me to use their stories and to those leaders whose wisdom I have drawn on in these pages.

Thanks to my bench of readers who gave me honest feedback on the drafts of this thing as it evolved: Rosie Fletcher, Jayma Pau, Jane Clubb, Craig Dearden Phillips and Johanna Campion. Hugely helpful.

Merci beaucoup Cleo Sheehan for your important intervention and creativity.

The cover of this book was designed by the very creative people at The Plant in London.

To Helen Coyle who got me unstuck on many occasions. What an editor she is.

I wouldn't have completed this book without the support and advice of Alison Jones, the founder of Practical Inspiration Publishing. She's great.

I have loved collaborating on the cartoons with the genius who is Hunt Emerson. Thanks mate. www.largecow.com.

And, of course, Maggie, for so much, for so long.

Index

Lightning Source UK Ltd.
Milton Keynes UK
UKHW020952060123
414924UK00014B/1710